Faith

THE ART OF LIVING SERIES
Series Editor: Mark Vernon

From Plato to Bertrand Russell philosophers have engaged wide audiences on matters of life and death. *The Art of Living* series aims to open up philosophy's riches to a wider public once again. Taking its lead from the concerns of the ancient Greek philosophers, the series asks the question "How should we live?". Authors draw on their own personal reflections to write philosophy that seeks to enrich, stimulate and challenge the reader's thoughts about their own life.

Published

Clothes   *John Harvey*
Death   *Todd May*
Deception   *Ziyad Marar*
Faith   *Theo Hobson*
Fame   *Mark Rowlands*
Hunger   *Raymond Tallis*
Illness   *Havi Carel*
Me   *Mel Thompson*
Middle Age   *Christopher Hamilton*
Pets   *Erica Fudge*
Sport   *Colin McGinn*
Wellbeing   *Mark Vernon*
Work   *Lars Svendsen*

Forthcoming

Commitment   *Piers Benn*
Empathy   *Roman Krznaric*
Forgiveness   *Eve Garrad & David McNaughton*
Money   *Eric Lonergan*
Self-Love   *John Lippitt*
Sex   *Seiriol Morgan*
Science   *Steve Fuller*

Faith

Theo Hobson

ACUMEN

For Tess: "And fatefully a new strain of / Faith formed ..."

First published in 2009 by Acumen

Acumen Publishing Limited
4 Saddler Street
Durham
DH1 3NP
www.acumenpublishing.co.uk

ISBN: 978-1-84465-202-0

British Library Cataloguing-in-Publication Data
A catalogue record for this book is available
from the British Library.

Typeset in Warnock Pro.
Printed in the UK by the MPG Books Group.

Contents

Introduction

"Why is he killing him?" This is what my four-year-old son asked me recently, with alarm. We were reading a children's version of the Bible. We had come to the story of Abraham and Isaac. Abraham is told by God to sacrifice his son Isaac, whom he loves. He starts to obey, and it is only when he is right on the verge of filicide that God changes his mind and calls it off. I had pondered the grim tale many times, and read the thoughts of various theologians and some horrified atheists. I had been fascinated by the nineteenth-century Danish thinker Søren Kierkegaard's line: the story should remind us that God is beyond human morality and rationality, that we have to trust him. It is the model for all faith. As I'll relate later on, this interpretation was an important influence on my own experience of Christian faith.

The shock of the story had become largely theoretical over the years, but now, reading it with my little boy, it felt fresh again. He was glancing up at me, demanding an explanation. "Why is he killing him?" I mumbled something about God playing a sort of trick on Abraham, but everything being all right in the end. If he were older I might have tried some Kierkegaard on him, or I might have taken an anthropological approach, and explained that ancient religion was tied up with human sacrifice, and that this story seems to mark a rejection of that. You can, to some extent, explain this story away. On the other hand, it is part of the Judaeo-Christian definition of faith. Judaism was founded when Abraham believed what God told him: that he would be the father of a great nation, through which all humanity would be blessed. He left his native land, and turned away from his native gods, in order to pursue this vision. It must have seemed like insanity to his contemporaries, but he trusted that this was God's master plan. And his trust was absolute, even overruling the paternal bond.

Why should anyone today choose to identify with this strange ancient character? That's the central question of this book: should we treat this business of faith with respect, or should we consign it to the troubled infancy of humanity, and move on? Or maybe we can secularize faith, purge it of its irrationalism? For faith in a more general sense is a virtue, surely? It is a near synonym of hope; it suggests a determination to see the potential in life, despite its difficulties, and there's a sense that this determination is hard-won, an inner struggle. Don't we all need faith of some sort? For life, as you may have noticed, is psychologically challenging; there are many good reasons for despondency, from personal worries to global warming. Will everything be all right? It seems unlikely – beyond unlikely. But we need to keep our spirits up. We need to trust that the world is not too hostile, that good and meaningful lives can be lived in it.

Of course it is always true that the world is a problem-ridden place, but at the time of writing, early 2009, it's more obvious than usual. We are in an economic downturn that might be a sustained depression. The outlook is bleak. In Britain, there is a grim sense that we have wasted a long period of economic growth, that we failed to make it serve the common good, that even in the good times we failed to become a happier, fairer society. Instead a mood of competitive anxiety deepened, and public culture became a bit nastier, more obsessed with money, sex and fame. The idea of the common good seemed to become more elusive. It's quite hard to feel optimistic about British society.

The same can be said about the global picture. In past decades, one could say that the world's poor were slowly being rescued by the march of industrial civilization. Trust in economic progress, and all will be well. But now, in a grim irony that is still sinking in, it seems that this "solution" contributes to an even larger problem: environmental disaster. Can we suddenly turn global politics around to avoid this? How on earth is one to feel moderately positive about the future of the planet?

To address these problems, we need a spirit of optimism, of hope. Of *faith*? That depends on what we mean by faith, the secular reader will reply. If it's a synonym of optimism and hope, then sure. But if it means the religious habit of preferring holy teaching to rational evidence, then no thanks. So surely my chief task, in introducing a book about faith, is to make it crystal clear which meaning of the word I shall tackle. But I cannot, for I believe that we can never clearly separate the religious from the non-religious meaning. Which is to say that "faith" cannot really be freed from its religious associations. Yes, to a large extent it can be used as a synonym of hope or optimism, but not entirely: a certain religious intensity comes through. Atheist writers, as we shall see, are aware of this, and so they tend to use "faith" in a strictly pejorative sense, to denote dangerous irrationalism. But this is falsely to narrow the concept of faith: to ignore its wider sense, which is stubbornly positive. The fact is that "faith" remains an attractive word, despite its irrational echoes.

Of course this wider sense of faith is vague: on the one hand it means the hopeful politics of people such as Barack Obama, whom we shall look at in Chapter 2, but it also means the everyday reality of people daring to be hopeful, telling themselves that the half-empty glass is half full. Faith in this wider sense is the psychological mechanism that enables us to cope with our awareness of the world's alarming downside, and show a positive face to the world. It is a special form of imagination: we assume a positive attitude by imagining a good future.

Couldn't we avoid religion-related confusion and call this *optimism* rather than faith? No, optimism is an inadequate word for what we are talking about, for it suggests either a natural quality that some are blessed with (there has recently been talk of locating an optimism gene), or a passing mood that we might experience from time to time. Optimism also suggests a certain reluctance to face the facts: a naivety, a penchant for rose-tinted eyewear. Faith is tougher. It knows the case for despair; it's more like courage-despite-realism; it implies a resisting, or temporary overcoming, of pessimism.

This is surely a near-universal human quality or experience: a positive attitude of existential courage. So why is it so hard to speak of, even to name? Perhaps because it's so important, and so personal. There's something presumptuous about speaking in general terms about it, as if one has an overview. And of course there's an added complication in the fact that the word "faith" is so closely associated with religion. The meaning of the concept exceeds religion, but the old religious associations echo through the word, and the implication that this bravely positive attitude is owned by religion denies it to atheists.

Consider a couple of examples. Imagine an idealistic teacher who puts a lot of effort into helping a difficult student, who repeatedly abuses that investment. We speak of the teacher having faith in the student. It is a shorthand way of saying that the teacher is admirably persistent, and willing to overlook evidence that the effort is not worthwhile (perhaps colleagues deride this persistence as naivety). And to say "I have faith in you" is a very strong affirmation: it is a promise to overlook past errors, to help someone to imagine his future working out well. Whether one likes it or not, the strength of the word, its ability to mean *really* determined optimism, is due to its religious history.

Or imagine a couple wondering whether to move house to an area where they will be in a racial and cultural minority. Will they feel part of the community? Will their children adapt, and get on at school? Their own parents and friends advise them to stay among their own and avoid unnecessary complications, telling them that it's too big a risk to take with their children's lives. The couple might decide: we know it's a risk, but one has to live with an attitude of faith. Here the meaning of faith is slightly different; it means trust that things will work out, a conviction that one's life decisions must not be made out of fear. So it means a principled attitude of trusting that all will be well.

In both of these cases faith describes an attitude that is suggestive of a whole worldview. We could use other words: the teacher is "hopeful" about the student, or "sees the potential" in him. But these words are a bit too ordinary: they don't convey the heroic, defiant, self-sacrificial quality of the teacher. And the couple is "optimistic", we could say "trusting", that their family will flourish. But again these words are not strong enough; they don't convey an imaginative leap, a defiance of playing it safe. Of course the teacher and the couple are not rejecting rationality, or the scientific method, but they are challenging "common sense", or "the reasonable view". This is important in relation to understanding the clash between faith and reason: reason is more than science, it also suggests convention, reasonability, realism.

Of course, faith is closely related to these other words: "hope", "trust" and "confidence". But these other words are more conventional, more prone to blandness, common sense, platitude. "Trust" is the particularly relevant word. Faith is a variant of trust, a strange mutation of it. Trust is a natural human characteristic; it makes society possible. Faith is an excess of trust; it stretches, or even defies, trust's grounding in reasonability. You could say that faith is trust's edgy little sister, who is dramatic, extravagant, over-the-top. If I let my wife go on a business trip with a colleague, that shows I trust her. If that trip lasts a month and I know the colleague to be a keen philanderer, then maybe we should speak of faith rather than trust. Faith could be defined as a form of trust that someone is laughing at. On the other hand, someone else might be admiring it.

So we could say this: faith is a form of trust that gets people talking. Faith is an intensification of trust that upsets trust's normal link to convention, reasonability.

So faith is a positive, hopeful attitude that is willing to dissent from convention, common sense, reasonability. It is a form of hope that sticks its neck out. But is this such a good thing? Not necessarily: there are great dangers here. The dramatic thrill of defying the common-sense view and striking out on one's own, following a vision: what could be more exciting, and more dangerous? From Shakespeare's villains and Milton's Satan through to Hitler, evil is keen to use the pathos of daring faith.

In the view of many, this danger discredits the supposed virtue of faith. Let us cease to idealize faith, and have a positive attitude to the social future that is rationally based. This sounds sensible, perhaps even obvious, but it overlooks the fact that faith seems to be more or less necessary to us, and that denying this is dangerous. The claim that we can have a positive attitude to the social future that is rationally based is naive. For rationality in the strict sense cannot substantiate this "positive attitude" as right. In other words, all talk of ideals and values has a faith dimension, and a "rational" ideology is bound to develop faith-like characteristics. This is perhaps the key insight of postmodern thought: we can no more ditch faith than we can jump away from our shadow.

This book is a reflection on the concept of faith, but it is less neutral than that sounds. Is it a defence of faith? No, the concept is too wide to be defended: Hitler's evil creed was a form of faith, and so was Karl Marx's "science". My approach is rooted in an argument about faith. I believe that we can only really understand the role of faith in modernity if we closely attend to the specifically Christian concept of faith. Part of my aim in what follows, then, is to give an account of Christian faith. This is not, or not just, a matter of sneaking in Christian apologetics to a book on a wider topic. It is because I do not think there could be a useful account of "faith in general". I cannot write about the concept of faith without making it clear what I think faith is meant to be.

The first chapter considers attitudes to faith in recent works of atheism: these authors focus on its irrational connotation, but do they also acknowledge that it refers to something admirable? The second chapter looks at the wider meaning of faith, using the examples of Obama's election, the economic crisis and the ever-topical issue of psychological angst. The third chapter returns to the religious meaning of faith, with an account of the theme of faith in the Bible. The fourth chapter looks for parallels in ancient Greek thought, and then looks at the tension between faith and reason in Christian thought, highlighting the "fideist" tradition that rejects a rational version of religion. This chapter also argues that huge areas of secular thought are moulded by this aspect of theology. Chapter 5 takes an autobiographical turn. I relate the way in which, as a student, I came to take faith seriously, and how I began to question what Christians are meant to have faith *in*. I was fascinated by the tense overlap of Christian and socialist idealism. It seemed to me that Christian faith entailed historical hope, akin to that of Marxism, but this raised a huge theological problem: how can a this-worldly Christianity avoid rationalist dilution and political dangers? Perhaps it must present itself as a form of utopianism, which differs from the Enlightenment varieties in never losing sight of the necessity of faith. The Conclusion notes that faith is both intellectually and psychologically problematic for the believer, yet the burden is light, for no other language of affirmation rings true.

1. Against faith

Recently I met a man at a party and we began talking about religion. I said I was a Christian. He asked me whether I had ever experienced serious doubts, whether my faith had ever been shaken. I tried to explain that it wasn't like that; that faith, in my experience, wasn't normally stable; that doubt and shakiness were sort of internal to it; that it was an endless argument with its opposite. Frankly I didn't much like the assumption behind his question: that my faith was probably something unexamined, vulnerable to a realism that I carefully shunned. Afterwards I realized how I should have replied. I should have asked him: have you ever questioned your assumption that you are a good person? He would probably have replied that he had never claimed to be a particularly good person. Well, I would have replied, I have never claimed that my faith is a stable possession.

My interlocutor had recently read Richard Dawkins's book *The God Delusion* (2006). Perhaps it had confirmed his assumption that religious faith is a flight from realism, from honesty. Of course, this book has a negative view of religious faith, but does it see any virtue in faith in a more general sense?

In what follows, I shall look at recent writings by Dawkins and three other atheists. There is a tendency for them to limit the meaning of "faith" to "religious faith", and belief's defiance of evidence and reason. There is almost no acknowledgement of the strange, awkward fact that the word has another meaning: trust, optimism, confidence, hope, a belief that the future will be all right, a belief in someone's ability to fulfil his potential. These atheists might say: that's another meaning of faith, which should be kept separate from religion. But that won't do. The two meanings are *not* completely separate; their overlap should be reflected on.

Dawkins tells us that his aim is to attack "anything and everything supernatural" (*ibid.*: 36), including every idea of God. He presents religion as the polar opposite of the scientific method, which makes rational arguments about evidence: "The whole point of religious faith, its strength and chief glory, is that it does not depend on rational justification. The rest of us are expected to defend our prejudices" (*ibid.*: 23). For him, it is easy to show that the God of the major religions does not exist. In early modern times, many thinkers proposed a rational sort of God, who keeps his distance from the world: "The deist God is certainly an improvement over the monster of the Bible" (*ibid.*: 46), but doesn't exist either. Can a scientist really enter this famously complex territory with such confidence? Yes: "the existence of God is a scientific hypothesis like any other … God's existence or non-existence is a scientific fact about the universe" (*ibid.*: 47).

Does atheism mean being absolutely certain that God doesn't exist? No, says Dawkins, for complete certainty is unavailable on this matter, and the atheist shouldn't fall into the trap of overplaying his hand. "It is in the nature of faith that one is capable … of holding a belief without adequate reason to do so … Atheists do not have faith; and reason alone could not propel one to total conviction that anything does not exist" (*ibid.*: 51). But this does not make him an agnostic: to see God's existence as very improbable, like that of fairies, is still atheism, he says. He attacks the idea that science and religion inhabit different spheres (especially scientist Stephen Jay Gould's claim that science and religion belong to "non-overlapping *magisteria*"). No, he says religion makes claims about the way the universe is, and science ought to argue against these claims.

He embarks on a long discussion of the "proofs" of God's existence, which gives the impression that these old monkish games are central to belief in God. Then he addresses the claim that many top scientists are believers. No, almost no good scientists are believers, he says, and he quotes a colleague who is astonished to meet any at all, "because I can't believe anyone accepts truth by revelation" (*ibid.*: 99).

He then asks why religion is so persistent. How has this gullibility evolved? It seems that human brains have evolved to be trusting of what they are told, and to be receptive to dualism (a belief in a mind–matter split) and to creationism. These traits, which have evolved for various reasons, allow religion its hold on us. But his big proposal is that religion is a collection of "memes" (ideas or cultural habits that work a bit like genes). One of these religion memes is as follows:

> Faith (belief without evidence) is a virtue. The more your beliefs defy the evidence, the more virtuous you are. Virtuoso believers who can manage to believe something really weird, unsupported and insupportable, in the teeth of evidence and reason, are especially highly rewarded. (*Ibid.*: 199)

A chapter on the Bible condemns the bad moral examples it contains, the moral madness that religious piety can involve. There's a punchy quotation from the scientist Steven Weinberg: "With or without [religion] you'd have good people doing good things and evil people doing evil things. But for good people to do evil things, it takes religion" (*ibid.*: 249).

In a section on religion and terrorism, he writes that it is a mistake to call terrorists evil: "They perceive their acts to be good, not because of some warped personal idiosyncrasy, and not because they have been possessed by Satan, but because they have been brought up, from the cradle, to have total and unquestioning *faith*" (*ibid.*: 304). And the problem does not lie just with "extremist" faith: all religion promotes the likelihood of violent extremism by teaching "that unquestioned faith is a virtue" (*ibid.*: 306). Of course, moderates call extremism a perversion of true faith, "but how can there be a perversion of faith, if faith, lacking objective justification, doesn't have any demonstrable standard to pervert?" The very concept of faith is a sort of poison, he maintains:

> Faith is an evil precisely because it requires no justification and brooks no argument. Teaching children that unquestioned faith is a virtue primes them – given certain other ingredients that are not hard to come by – to grow up into potentially lethal weapons for future jihads or crusades ... Faith can be very very dangerous, and deliberately to implant it into the vulnerable mind of an innocent child is a grievous wrong. (*Ibid.*: 308)

So how does Dawkins use the word "faith"? Sometimes it is a synonym for "religion", but more often it refers to that aspect of religion that legitimizes irrationality and demeans evidence-based knowledge. It is a sort of mechanism whereby believers override the claims of evidence in order to stick with holy teachings. To his disgust, modern society tolerates this mechanism. "If somebody announces that [something] is part of his *faith*, the rest of society, whether of the same faith, or another, or of none, is obliged, by ingrained custom, to 'respect' it without question" (*ibid.*: 306). So faith seems to be a form of irrationalism that, thanks to the indulgence of society, has an aura of justification, even nobility.

Does he have a sort of faith himself? He certainly has a sort of idealism: on the first page he says he hopes that his book will free some of its readers from the bondage of religion, and he also offers us a vision of a better world: "Imagine, with John Lennon, a world without religion" (*ibid.*: 1). This possible world, of course, is defined by the absence of religion-related violence. In that song, Lennon explicitly links atheism with a sort of utopian idealism. Dawkins tentatively echoes this.

The rise of atheist polemics over the past few years has been a transatlantic phenomenon. Sam Harris got there a couple of years before Dawkins with *The End of Faith: Religion, Terror and the Future of Reason* (2004). His tone is grave. Religion will wipe us out, if we let it. We *must* move on from it, as we moved on from old errors such as alchemy. "Faith-based religion must suffer the same slide into obsolescence" (Harris 2004: 14). The phrase "faith-based religion" is significant: Harris defends the quest for spiritual meaning, as long it is fully compatible with reason. "We cannot live by reason alone. This is why no quantity of reason, applied as antiseptic, can compete with the balm of faith, once the terrors of this world begin to intrude upon our lives" (*ibid.*: 43). We need to develop a rational spirituality to help us cope with life. And to this end we need to reject religion in its present form: "every religion preaches the truth of propositions for which no evidence is even *conceivable*" (*ibid.*: 23). We have erred in tolerating this for so long: the world is in peril owing to "the concessions we have made to religious faith – to the idea that belief can be sanctified by something other than *evidence*" (*ibid.*: 9); "we must find our way to a time when faith, without evidence, disgraces anyone who would claim it" (*ibid.*: 48). The idea of moderate, reasonable faith is an illusion: the terrorists of 9/11 were "men of faith – *perfect* faith, as it turns out – and this, it must be finally acknowledged, is a terrible thing to be" (*ibid.*: 67).

Why is this unreason so persistent? As he has already suggested, faith is fuelled by our fear of "the terrors of this world", especially death. "Without death, the influence of faith-based religion would be unthinkable … faith is little more than the shadow cast by our hope for a better life beyond the grave" (*ibid.*: 39).

Harris has a long section on the nature of belief in which he shows far more philosophical curiosity than Dawkins. Indeed, at the risk of offending him, he shows some degree of theological curiosity. He even bothers considering the etymology of "faith". There is a passage worth quoting at length:

The Hebrew term *'emûnâ* (verb *'mn*) is alternately translated as "to have faith", "to believe", or "to trust". The Septuagint, the Greek translation of the Hebrew Bible, retains the same meaning in the term *pisteuein*, and this Greek equivalent is adopted in the New Testament. Hebrews 11:1 defines faith as "the assurance of things hoped for, the conviction of things not seen". Read in the right way, this passage seems to render faith entirely self-justifying: perhaps the very fact that one believes in something which has not yet come to pass ("things hoped for") or for which one has no evidence ("things not seen") constitutes evidence for its actuality ("assurance"). Let's see how this works: I feel a certain, rather thrilling "conviction" that Nicole Kidman is in love with me. As we have never met, my feeling is my only evidence of her infatuation. I reason thusly: my feelings suggest that Nicole and I must have a special, even metaphysical, connection – otherwise, how could I have this feeling in the first place? I decide to set up camp outside her house to make the necessary introductions; clearly, this sort of faith is a tricky business.

Throughout this book, I am criticizing faith in its ordinary, scriptural sense – as belief in, and life orientation toward, certain historical and metaphysical propositions. The meaning of the term, both in the Bible and upon the lips of the faithful, seems to be entirely unambiguous … Religious faith is simply *unjustified* belief in matters of ultimate concern – specifically in propositions that promise some mechanism by which human life can be spared the ravages of time and death. *(Ibid.*: 64–5)

We shall return to this passage once we've looked at the Bible, for it epitomizes the common habit of these atheists of narrowing the meaning of faith. A few pages further on, he approaches the essence of faith slightly differently:

> Where faith really pays dividends … is in the conviction that the future will be better than the past, or at least not worse. Consider the celebrated opinion of Julian of Norwich (ca. 1342–1413), who distilled the message of the Gospels in the memorable sentence "All shall be well, and all shall be well, and all manner of thing shall be well." The allure of most religious doctrines is nothing more sublime or inscrutable than this: *things will turn out well in the end*. Faith is offered as a means by which the truth of this proposition can be savored in the present and secured in the future.   (*Ibid.*: 69–70)

I would like to know what Harris thinks *is* really sublime and inscrutable. I cannot think of anything "higher" than a person in near despair determining to go on, feeling that, despite the evidence, life will be good. Anyway, this is an important insight into the nature of faith, particularly Christian faith. It is indeed all about this vision of future well-being. But does this square with his earlier claim that the essential religious motivation is fear of death? A lazy thinker would say: well, it's all wishful thinking, whether the emphasis is on personal death-survival or some vague utopia. But there are different forms of wishful thinking, from hoping your enemy magically dies to hoping that world peace breaks out. Harris should be clearer about the nature of the wishful thinking he thinks underlies faith. To root it all in the desire for consolation in the face of personal annihilation will not do, if a key part of the motivation is the desire for some sort of cosmic utopia. These ideals might overlap but let us not pretend they are the same thing. In his epilogue he says that faith makes people "eager to sacrifice happiness, compassion, and justice in this world, for a fantasy of a world to come" (*ibid.*: 223). But this sort of dualism is explicitly absent from the Julian of Norwich quote: "all manner of thing" sounds to me like a very general hope, inclusive of this world. If we are to think and speak intelligently about religion, we must attend to what religious language *actually says*, rather than assume we already know what it really means.

In an odd final chapter he advocates an expansion of consciousness through rational mysticism. It resembles a New Age tract gone astray. "While spiritual experience is clearly a natural propensity of the human mind, we need not believe anything on insufficient evidence to actualize it" (*ibid.*: 221). This new approach to spirituality would entail "the end of faith". In the epilogue he calls faith "the devil's masterpiece" (*ibid.*: 226).

Like Dawkins, Harris exhibits a certain idealism. He believes that the world can be saved from destruction if faith is knocked from its pedestal. Early on he says, "what follows is written very much in the spirit of a prayer" (*ibid.*: 29). He exhibits an idealism that is related to faith, in one sense of the word. At the very end of the book Harris says that without God we can "realize, one fine day, that we do, in fact, love our neighbours, that their happiness is inextricable from our own, and that our interdependence demands that people everywhere be given the opportunity to flourish". Fact or prayer?

A similar approach to faith is evident in *God is Not Great*, by Christopher Hitchens (2007). He begins with a couple of childhood memories, including some words from his headmaster. "'You might not see the point of all this faith now,' he said. 'But you will one day, when you start to lose loved ones'" (2007: 4). This immediately struck him as a dubious defence of religion, and still does. He soon returns to the issue: "As for consolation, since religious people so often insist that faith answers this supposed need, I shall simply say that those who offer false consolation are false friends" (*ibid.*: 9). He concludes the opening chapter by returning to our hunger for consolation: "Religious faith is, precisely *because* we are still-evolving creatures, ineradicable. It will never die out, or at least not until we get over our fear of death, and of the dark, and of the unknown, and of each other" (*ibid.*: 12). Later he returns to the consolation theme: "In *The Future of an Illusion*, Freud made the obvious point that religion suffered from one incurable deficiency: it was too clearly derived from our own desire to escape from or survive death" (*ibid.*: 103).

Atheism is not an alternative faith, he says. "Our belief is not a belief. Our principles are not a faith. We do not rely solely upon science and reason, because these are necessary rather than sufficient factors, but we distrust anything that contradicts science or outrages reason" (*ibid.*: 5). Not only does religion dare to contradict science, but it claims an inappropriate degree of certainty. "The person who is certain, and who claims divine warrant for his certainty, belongs now to the infancy of our species" (*ibid.*: 11). This mental infant is dangerous: here Hitchens ponders the events of 11 September 2001. "The nineteen suicide murderers of New York and Washington and Pennsylvania were without any doubt the most sincere believers on those planes" (*ibid.*: 32).

Like Harris, he shows some theological curiosity. In the past, faith made grand attempts to justify itself rationally, but faith of the "sort that can stand up at least for a while in a confrontation with reason is now plainly impossible" (*ibid.*: 63). As the nineteenth-century French thinker Pierre Simon Laplace said, we have no need for the God hypothesis. Hitchens says that astute theologians always knew this, and insisted that belief in God was totally dependent on faith. But such astuteness is self-defeating: "If one must have faith in order to believe something, or believe *in* something, then the likelihood of that something having any truth or value is considerably diminished" (*ibid.*: 71). Thinkers including Kierkegaard tried to make a virtue of the "leap of faith" that defies evidence, but this leap "is actually too much for the human mind, and leads to delusions and manias" (*ibid.*), which is why religion generally falls back on its pseudo-rational proofs.

Like Dawkins, Hitchens calls religious faith absurdly unnecessary, for the world as it really is inspires wonder. He quotes Albert Einstein: "If something is in me which can be called religious then it is the unbounded admiration for the structure of the world so far as our science can reveal it" (quoted in *ibid.*: 278). To prefer "dogma and faith over doubt and experiment is to throw out the ripening vintage and to reach greedily for the Kool-Aid" (*ibid.*). (Dawkins is very big on this sort of rhetoric: he loves to quote Charles Darwin's conclusion to *On the Origin of Species*: "there is grandeur in this view of life", quietly widening the reference of "this view" from evolution to atheism.)

So faith is a sort of violence practised on oneself and others: those who "claim to know the truth of revelation ... are deceiving themselves and attempting to deceive – or to intimidate – others" (*ibid.*: 278). This sketch of the believer's motivation seems a bit ungenerous. Surely there is also moral idealism, the desire to change the world? Hitchens knows about a version of such idealism: he used to be a believer in Marxism. Was this a sort of faith? He thinks not:

> When I was a Marxist, I did not hold my opinions as a matter of faith but I did have the conviction that a sort of unified field theory might have been discovered. The concept of historical and dialectical materialism was not an absolute and it did not have any supernatural element, but it did have its messianic element in the idea that an ultimate moment might arrive ...
>
> (*Ibid.*: 151)

In the end his attempt to believe in this political creed was defeated by his acceptance of reality, he says. But he sometimes misses his former convictions, "as if they were an amputated limb". What is interesting here is that he refuses to put Marxism in the "faith" category, despite its "messianic element". In effect he is saying, let us restrict the word "faith" to supernatural belief systems that rely on spurning rationality. And he is refusing to notice that one aspect of religious faith is precisely the messianic hope that attracted him to Marxism.

Can he not admit that some religious believers seem motivated by idealism rather than bullying, or the need for consolation? In a previous book he wrote: "I have met many brave men and women, morally superior to myself, whose courage in adversity derives from their faith" (Hitchens 2001: 56). Maybe his dislike of religion is partly rooted in the former believer's envy of those who retain allegiance to a bold belief system, and overarching narrative of purpose.

He finishes with a burst of idealism: a new Enlightenment could go a long way to seeing religion off. This would lead to better science, and a fuller liberation of sex from old tyrannies. "And all this and more is, for the first time in our history, within the reach if not the grasp of everyone" (*ibid.*: 283).

Hitchens repeatedly roots faith in the need for consolation; it is fuelled by "our fear of death, and of the dark, and of the unknown, and of each other". Our fear of these things tempts us to cling to illusions. But there is another way of looking at this. These fears are not silly childish delusions: they are real, normal, universal. We must arm ourselves against these fears, take courage. And faith is a way of doing so. From one perspective, religion is simply realistic about human vulnerability; it is honest about our deepest existential fears in a way that secular discourse tends not to be. Hitchens's refusal of this perspective feels like adolescent prejudice: he would not reject poetry on the grounds that it is a response to death and the unknown.

Also published in 2007 was a short collection of anti-religion essays by the British philosopher A. C. Grayling: *Against All Gods*. "Faith is a commitment to belief contrary to evidence and reason, as between them Kierkegaard and the tale of Doubting Thomas are at pains to show" (2007: 15). It is belief in the absence of evidence, "or even (to the greater merit of the believer) in the very teeth of evidence contrary to that belief" (*ibid.*: 34–5). This is not worthy of respect: "On the contrary: to believe something in the face of evidence and against reason – to believe something by faith – is ignoble, irresponsible and ignorant, and merits the opposite of respect" (*ibid.*: 16).

He angrily denies the charge made by some believers that atheism is also a faith position: "People who do not believe in supernatural entities do not have a 'faith' in the non-existence of [these entities]" (*ibid.*: 34). They simply respond to the evidence. Yet sometimes his tetchy atheism seems to entail something like faith. A few pages later he claims that in the absence of religion we could:

> have a proper discussion about the ethical principles of mutual concern, imaginative sympathy and courageous tolerance on which the chances for individual and social flourishing rest. We need to meet one another as human individuals, person to person, in a public domain hospitable to us all, independently of the Babel of divisive labels people impose on others or adopt for themselves. Look at children in nursery school: a real effort has to be made to teach them, later on, how to put up barriers between themselves and their classmates on the basis of gender, ethnicity and their parents' choice of superstition. That is how our tragedy as a species is kept going: in the systematic perversion of our first innocence by falsehood and factionalism. (*Ibid.*: 38–9)

In other words, *Imagine there's no heaven …* The lack of self-awareness is funny. Although he is right that the rejection of religion is not in itself a "faith", he goes on to demonstrate that the rejection of religion *as the thing that holds back the world from peace and harmony* looks rather faith based. Or does he have evidence of a post-religious utopia, of post-theistic humanity becoming naturally good? He displays a trust that if religion is got rid of, humanity can be its best self, a new age can dawn. This echoes Lennon's song, *but he was more honest,* for he admitted that campaigning atheism entails a utopian idealism: a belief that the world could be made new when this stain is removed. Grayling seems motivated by this vision, but unaware of the faith it entails.

"The non-rational mindset underlying religious belief [is] an essentially infantile attitude of acceptance of fairy-stories" (*ibid.*: 43). Humanism, which Grayling asserts is the alternative to religious belief, is wiser: "In contrast to the utter certainties of faith, a humanist has a humbler conception of the nature and current extent of knowledge" (*ibid.*: 63). And humanism is braver: "Its desire to learn from the past, its exhortation to courage in the present, and its espousal of hope for the future, are about real things, real people, real human need and possibility, and the fact of the fragile world we share" (*ibid.*: 64). Note that for Grayling the rejection of religion is not a neutral, value-free attitude, a mere negative, but better at supplying the things that religion tries to: courage, hope, possibility. He chooses not to notice that these qualities are related to faith.

So all these atheists dislike religious faith on the grounds that it is contrary to evidence and reason. Are they right about this? On one level, yes of course, but on closer inspection this is a very complex question. It is true that religious faith entails saying things that cannot be backed up by evidence, things that *seem* to imply disdain for science and rationality. When I say the Lord's Prayer, am I indulging in irrationalism? Of course, says the atheist, for my words imply that this being exists and hears, and can deliver me from evil and so on. But the strange thing is this: my saying of this prayer is compatible with my acceptance of what scientists and rationalists say – *until they start saying the world would be better off if people stopped praying*. Faith is defiant of a strictly rational worldview, but is not therefore actively inimical to science or rationality. Of course it can be inimical, as is the case with creationism, but it is not *necessarily* so. My point is that the question of whether religion rejects reason is one that must be handled with great care and attention to the complex facts rather than the sweeping use of a blunt theory.

The tendency of the four atheists I have discussed here to limit the meaning of "faith" to a defiance of evidence and reason has lost sight of the overlapping meaning: trust, confidence and hope. Of course it is not in the atheists' interest to acknowledge this more benign meaning of "faith", for the reader might start thinking that there is something more to religious faith than blind irrationalism: that it inspires hope.

This evasion is ironic in the light of the idealism that lingers in the background of strident atheism. While attacking faith in one sense, they exhibit a sort of faith, in the other sense. For they display a trust that things can be radically better.

I want to remind these atheists that faith, in the religious sense, is related to faith in the wider sense. The religious believer is attracted to religion's ability to supply hope, affirmation – on a personal and a social level. The fact that many intelligent people continue to be religious shows that the attraction of faith outweighs the intellectual difficulties. One's desire to participate in this mythical narrative, of God putting life right, is so strong that one's idea of "truth" widens, and the seeming irrationality of faith becomes something one can live with. The atheist may reply: but you don't *need* this mythical narrative; you can affirm life in a purely secular way; you can have a "good attitude" without religion. But the believer opts to affirm life in *this* way, in this ancient language of total hope; he says that "good attitude" is encoded in this tradition.

The growing atheist movement of the past few years has, at the time of writing, taken a curious new route. Some London buses, including many of my local ones, carry an advertisement reading: "There is probably no God. Now stop worrying and enjoy your life". The websites of a humanist society and of Richard Dawkins are placed underneath. It is interesting that the campaigners have chosen to associate atheism with mild hedonism. Because God (probably) does not exist, have a good time, put personal contentment first. The "probably" has been widely criticized as a cop-out; I

21

think it is unwittingly eloquent of what atheism is about. For it associates atheism with playing it safe, conformity, pragmatism, and so by implication associates God with what is unlikely, surprising, adventurous. So this advertising campaign unwittingly suggests that there is something rather romantic about faith. As we shall soon see, "improbable" is one of Obama's favourite words. I am reminded of something the novelist John Updike once said about religion: "Among the repulsions of atheism for me has been its drastic uninterestingness as an intellectual position" (Updike 1983: 135).

2. What else is faith?

I've argued so far that the atheists who denigrate faith as dangerous, as "the devil's masterpiece", in Harris's words (2004: 226), look away from an interesting complication. Even people who are not in the least religious are in the habit of using the word in a positive way. In this chapter we shall look at some of the non-religious associations of "faith": in politics, economics and psychology. With the financial crisis that began in September 2008, and the election of Barack Obama to the US presidency, the news in recent months has been dominated by the need for faith, and the role of faith in political life.

Faith, hope and Obama

I could not be writing this at a better moment. Earlier this week Barack Obama was inaugurated as the forty-fourth president of the United States of America. Two million people congregated in Washington, DC, and much of the rest of the world watched on television.

As his campaign for presidential election hotted-up in 2008, it became clear that Obama was something out of the ordinary. There was a cultic element to his following, and to his mantra: "Yes we can". He was forging a new politics of enthusiasm, in the literal sense of religious excitement, and this wasn't limited to his own country; much of the rest of the world was carried along. And this was intensified by the new uncertainty unleashed by the economic crisis: the world seemed to need strong moral leadership more obviously than usual. So it began to seem that this man embodied political idealism in a more ambitious way, a more convincing way, than I had ever seen. He has become the focus for our attempts to be hopeful about the world situation.

Over the past few days the British press has left cynicism aside. A leading article in the *Independent on Sunday* said: "Nobody expects him to transform everything, but we really can hope that a new US president, of good heart and cool head, will summon us to make the world a better place. In our time" (*Independent* 2009). Andrew Rawnsley, writing in the *Observer*, agreed: "He is giving his country, and many people beyond it, a much needed injection of optimism just by being there. He wields words with power – not a talent to be dismissed when an insecure world looks for inspiration" (Rawnsley 2009).

On the day of inauguration, journalistic idealism reached a new pitch. In the *Guardian* Polly Toynbee wrote: "As that inauguration speech echoes out, the globe itself seems to inhale a mighty, collective intake of breath, frighteningly audacious in its hope". Democratic politics has been uninspiring for decades, she observes:

> But now Obama comes out of nowhere just when good politics has never mattered more .... If ever the world needed saving, it's now. So here comes the man who says he can ... The hope is not just for what the man will do, but that his brand of politics rubs off on politicians everywhere ... This is the day to honour the practice of politics as a high calling, where the power to inspire can swell the hearts of the world.
> (Toynbee 2009)

He sounds like the icon of a global secular faith. Toynbee is no fan of religion, so it might seem that Obama is the icon for secular progressives, for post-Christian idealism. But his idealism didn't look very post-Christian on Tuesday. The inauguration was a remarkable television event. The crowd on Capitol Hill was so large that it was hard to believe it was not computer-generated. They were standing there on this freezing morning to witness a powerful ritual. On one level it was a secular ritual: the handover of power, the welcoming of a new leader. But it was also a religious ceremony, one of the biggest in history. In a sense it was rather like a church wedding: a religious ceremony with such an important secular function that one is apt to be a bit surprised when the vicar starts referring to God. The pastor who said the inaugural prayers, Rick Warren, was like an unexpectedly charismatic vicar at a wedding. This "religious bit" isn't ceremonial background, his big voice insisted. There was no retreat behind antique religious language, as you get in Britain's grand occasions of state. There was plainness, directness, sincerity: a shocking lack of shame about public religion.

Obama's speech was carefully sober, showing that his rhetoric was shifting from campaigning mode to governing mode. Like all good sermons it set out the problem (the economic crisis and the sense of a sapping of American confidence) with slightly worrying realism, awkwardly brutal honesty. And then it gradually moved the curative rhetoric into gear. Towards the end there were echoes of Isaiah: "old hatreds shall someday pass", we must work for "a new era of peace". These prophetic echoes were repeated by the minister who said the final prayers: he hoped that tanks would be turned into tractors, and quoted the Old Testament's most emotive line of all, about God's righteousness covering the earth like the waters cover the sea.

Despite the constitutional separation of church and state, America is glad to assert that religion and politics are joined at the hip, that national politics is renewed by means of religion. But in recent decades this overlap of religion and politics fell into disrepair, and became a cause of disunity, owing to the ascendancy of the religious right. Obama has unseated this force, and revived the nation's old liberal, progressive religious tradition. He has done so by placing himself in the civil rights tradition, which is more religious than mainstream politics. This tradition is defined by a rhetorical blurring of religion and politics. The speeches of Martin Luther King are the template for this: he was a preacher rather than a politician. Of course there is also a blurring of religion and politics on the right, but the civil rights tradition can do this blurring in a nation-including way, rather than a partisan way.

This, then, was the genius of his campaign: to bring the civil rights version of religious politics into the mainstream. Many would have assumed that this tradition is too marginal, too partisan to build a national campaign on, but this is wrong: this tradition is actually in tune with the national myth − it can be "scaled up" to fit it. This seems to have been his conscious plan from the start of his campaign: when he declared his candidacy in February 2007, he gave a quick sketch of American history, culminating in King, and his "call to let justice roll down like water, and righteousness like a mighty stream" (Obama 2008: 206). Throughout the nation's history, "a new generation has risen up and done what's needed to be done. Today we are called once more − and it is time for our generation to answer that call" (*ibid.*). He finally refers to his candidacy as "this improbable quest", and says he sees "a future of endless possibility stretching before us" (*ibid.*: 211).

"Hope" became his key concept, his banner, his endlessly repeated mantra. In January 2008 he spoke on the theme in Iowa. He explained how it was basic to his campaign, and then paused for reflection:

> For many months, we've been teased, even derided, for talking about hope. But we always knew that hope is not blind optimism. It's not ignoring the enormity of the task ahead or the roadblocks that stand in our path … Hope is that thing inside

us that insists, despite all evidence to the contrary, that something better awaits us if we have the courage to reach for it,
and to work for it, and to fight for it.   (*Ibid.*: 216)

Hope, he goes on, "is the bedrock of this nation". In some ways
it sounds more like faith, especially when it defies evidence. But
of course "hope" is less troubling to secular ears than "faith". The
fact that "hope" can suggest "faith" in a way that pleases religious
hearers yet does not offend secular ones is absolutely key to his
rhetorical success.

A few days later in New Hampshire he referred to his campaign
as "our improbable journey". The phrase suggests reliance on God's
miracle, Abraham-like obedience to God's crazy call. He says he
has been warned against offering people false hope: "But in the
unlikely story that is America, there has never been anything false
about hope" (*ibid.*: 222). And now he sums up the "simple creed"
of the nation: "Yes we can", a phrase repeated eight times in the rest
of the text.

In March, in Philadelphia, he referred to America's "improbable
experiment in democracy", before moving on to the race issue. He
can promise no swift resolution of the problem, he says. "But I have
asserted a firm conviction – a conviction rooted in my faith in God
and my faith in the American people – that working together we
can move beyond some of our old racial wounds" (*ibid.*: 236).

In June he spoke in a Chicago church about fatherhood and
hope.

> I'm not talking about an idle hope that's little more than blind
> optimism or willful ignorance of the problems we face. I'm
> talking about hope as that spirit inside us that insists, despite
> all evidence to the contrary, that something better is waiting
> for us if we're willing to work for it and fight for it. If we are
> willing to believe.   (*Ibid.*: 250)

Again, it sounds like faith, under the cover of a less contentious word.

In July he spoke in Berlin, so widening his message beyond his own nation. He concluded that "we are heirs to a struggle for freedom. We are a people of improbable hope" (*ibid.*: 281). The "we" is vague – the free world, perhaps. There is an echo of St Paul, who said that we are "heirs" to God's Old Testament promise.

On election night he gave his victory speech to an amazed throng in Chicago. It can no longer be doubted, he began, "that America is a place where all things are possible; [that] the dream of our founders is alive in our time" (*ibid.*: 283). We must answer cynicism and doubt with "that timeless creed that sums up the spirit of a people: Yes we can" (*ibid.*: 289).

His achievement was to bring out the inner affinity of the American story and Christian faith, and to do so without scaring secular liberals. But to do so with such force takes more than cunning spin skills; he had to put the force of his character and life story behind his message. So how did he come to combine religious and political faith with such assurance? Which came first?

In 1995, before entering politics, he published the memoir *Dreams from My Father*. It is a vivid depiction of the extended adolescent aloneness that his mixed-race origin entailed. To be of indeterminate identity is to suffer a sort of curse, to belong nowhere. He cannot help aspiring to white culture, for it is so closely identified with success and intellectual refinement. Yet authenticity feels black. As a student he puts a toe into the waters of civil rights activism. When a fellow student, a black girl called Regina, congratulates him on a rousing speech he has given, he says he feels a fraud. She tells him not to be so self-regarding: the cause is what matters. "It's about people who need your help. Children who are depending on you." He scoffs at the idealism, offending her. Another friend comes up and asks him what all that was about. "'Nothing', I said … 'She just believes in things that aren't really there'" (2007: 110).

He ponders this later, while listening to Billie Holiday. "Her voice sounded different to me now. Beneath the layers of hurt, beneath the ragged laughter, I heard a willingness to endure. Endure – and make music that wasn't there before" (*ibid.*: 112).

This is his turning-point, his "call". It might sound over the top, but I think there is an echo of the Moses story. Moses realized he didn't belong to the Egyptian court in which he was raised, that his true identity lay with his own people – yet simply moving from court to ghetto was impossible, and inauthentic. His self-realization demanded political transformation: the liberation of the enslaved Jews. I have no idea whether Obama had this template in mind when writing his book (what hubris if he did!), but it's certainly there. His true belonging cannot be to any presently existing entity – only to a possible future one, and the movement that works for it. The above passage contains two references to faith: the girl believes in things that aren't there, and he hears in the song a pathos of visionary endurance. His long-sought identity has to be faith based.

The paradox is that his semi-detachment from black identity intensifies his attachment to the civil rights vision. Were he fully African-American, he could more easily settle for the status quo, resign himself to the nation's divided culture. His psychological unease demands change. His only possible belonging is to the movement for change. He starts dwelling on his mental images of the civil rights movement: defiant protesters, election organizers, and "a county jail bursting with children, their hands clasped together, singing freedom songs":

Such images became a form of prayer for me, bolstering my spirits, channeling my emotions in a way that words never could. They told me … that I wasn't alone in my particular struggles, and that communities had never been a given in this country, at least not for blacks. Communities had to be created, fought for, tended like gardens. They expanded or contracted with the dreams of men – and in the civil rights movement those dreams had been large. In the sit-ins, the marches, the jailhouse songs, I saw the African-American community becoming more than just the place where you'd been born or the house where you'd been raised. Through organizing, through shared sacrifice, membership had been earned. And because membership was earned – because this community I imagined was still in the making, built on the promise that the larger American community, black, white, and brown, could somehow redefine itself – I believed that it might, over time, admit the uniqueness of my own life.   (*Ibid.*: 134–5)

The hopeful insight is that cultural belonging is not static. This passage is a rebuttal of so much of modern thought, which sees authenticity in roots, soil, organic tradition, in the attempt to be authentic Scots, or Serbs, or Jews. No, says Obama, let's locate authentic belonging in a vision of what might be. And this insight is possible for him because the African-American tradition reached a height of authenticity when it looked radically forwards and outwards, instead of (as is normal in the search for identity) backwards and inwards. How did it do this? How did it buck the logic of identity politics in this way? Through the fullness of its debt to Judaeo-Christian faith.

So the civil rights movement is for him a secular faith, a political faith. Except it's not: it is rooted in religion. Obama, being at this point an agnostic, doesn't want to focus on these roots. He starts his organizing job in Chicago, which is mostly about getting churches involved in politics. The churches in his area are largely Catholic, and run by white priests (the congregations have become increasingly black owing to white flight). He is wary of religion, for poor blacks need to find strength in unity, and countless competing denominations don't seem to help. The golden age of the civil rights movement rose above petty sectarianism, he observes: how could that spirit be revived? His thought is sharpened by an encounter with the Nation of Islam movement, urging blacks to purist separatism. His own hybridity makes this unappealing, and he renews his idealism in the civil rights movement as inclusive, nation-wide. He is soon visited by his Kenyan sister and learns more about his late father ("the Old Man"), and is disenchanted: when his American life didn't work out Obama senior had become angry, embittered, hopeless. The ghostly authority of his father is exorcized. His father was Muslim, so the idea deepens in Obama's mind that the Muslim-purist version of black politics is the wrong approach.

He meets an old black Protestant minister who sharpens his interest in the Christian origins of the civil rights movement. Obama admits that he is not really rooted in any particular church. This might put off some church leaders, whose support Obama seeks, says the minister. "What you're asking from pastors requires us to set aside some of our more priestly concerns in favour of prophecy. That requires a good deal of faith on our part. It makes us want to know just where you're getting yours from. Faith, that is" (*ibid.*: 274). He ponders this later on. Real commitment to the cause did indeed require faith; where did he get his? "It suddenly occurred to me that I didn't have an answer. Perhaps, still, I had faith in myself. But faith in one's self was never enough" (*ibid.*: 279).

He meets more black Protestant ministers and is impressed by their "confidence", and "certainty of purpose" (*ibid.*). He discovers Reverend Wright's church, which seems an ideal classless black community. He is impressed by many people in this church, but "I remained a reluctant skeptic, doubtful of my own motives, wary of expedient conversion" (*ibid.*: 286–7). And then he hears Wright preach a sermon on hope, on the Christian impulse to praise God even in the midst of pain. Amid an emotional congregation, Obama confronts "the desire to give oneself up to a God that could somehow put a floor on despair" (*ibid.*: 294). And he felt part of a larger movement:

I imagined the stories of ordinary black people merging with the stories of David and Goliath, Moses and Pharaoh, the Christians [*sic*] in the lion's den, Ezekiel's field of dry bones. Those stories – of survival, and freedom, and hope – became our story, my story ... Our trials and triumphs became at once unique and universal, black and more than black ... I felt for the first time how [this church's] spirit carried within it, nascent, incomplete, the possibility of moving beyond our narrow dreams.   (*Ibid.*)

For Christians, the Old Testament is the story of a very particular people that has totally universal relevance. What Obama sees is that the black American story is the same: it belongs to a particular people, yet its meaning spills out beyond this, seeks universality – its idea of liberation is a general, utopian thing. And this is because it is saturated in the Bible. It is because of its debt to the Bible that the civil rights movement can be simultaneously authentically black *and* not limited by this, not proudly purist, open to the whiter world. This solves his own conundrum.

Before he hears this sermon he certainly has a sort of faith: in the renewability of the civil rights movement. But it is unsettled, it is anxiously uncertain about its nature: is it a search for black authenticity, or is it a wider liberal thing? Is it religious or secular?

At the end of the book he weeps at his father's grave, and at his story. His journey from Kenya to Hawaii brought guilt that he was abandoning his traditions, selling out. This ruined his chances in America, and so he returned to Africa proud and embittered. He should have known that his journey from the African village to America entailed faith: "a faith born out of hardship, a faith that wasn't new, that wasn't black or white or Christian or Muslim but that pulsed in the heart of the first African village and the first Kansas homestead – a faith in other people" (*ibid.*: 429). In other words, the difficulty of moving from one world to another, of negotiating globalized modernity, is so great, and the dangers of pride and insecurity are so strong, that faith is indispensable.

Does it matter what sort of faith? Does it matter in what myth the faith is based? The above passage implies not: faith is a general human aptitude. But most of the book has been implying that the rooting of faith does matter. Obama has struggled to understand himself, and his vague faith in political change, and has come to see that his "civil rights faith" has an intrinsically Judaeo-Christian shape; it is this inheritance that allows it to be both particular and universal.

Eleven years later, in 2006, as a senator, he gave a talk in which he touched on his religious development. He grew up with "a healthy skepticism of organized religion", he says.

> And if it weren't for the particular attributes of the historically black church, I may have accepted this fate ... In its histor-ical struggles for freedom and the rights of man, I was able to see faith as more than just a comfort to the weary or a hedge against death, but rather as an active, palpable agent in the world. As a source of hope.   (Obama 2006)

There is a proper overlap of religious and political rhetoric, he goes on:

> [I]f we scrub [political] language of all religious content, we forfeit the imagery and terminology through which millions of Americans understand both their personal morality and social justice. Imagine Lincoln's Second Inaugural Address without reference to "the judgements of the Lord". Or King's I Have a Dream speech without references to "all of God's chil-dren". Their summoning of a higher truth helped inspire what had seemed impossible, and move the nation to embrace a common destiny.   (*Ibid.*)

33

Obama's great achievement, so far, has been to tap in to the founding faith of his nation, to reactivate it. And this form of faith directly contradicts the assumption that religious faith is one thing, and political faith another. In this case the overlap is undeniable.

Faith and capitalism

While Obama was promising to renew faith in the American idea, an aspect of that idea was looking shaky. The banking crisis, or credit crunch, was hovering in the background, and then in September 2008 the crash came, with various famous banks collapsing.

For years the banks had encouraged an explosion of credit, and allowed bad debt to multiply and infect the whole system. The assumption was that a growing economy could easily accommodate a few bad debts, but instead these "toxic" debts burst the banking bubble. The banks stopped believing in the worth of the financial products that they sold to each other. They therefore suffered a crisis of confidence in the whole game they had been playing. This was disastrous for the wider economy, which relies on banks lending to each other, trusting each other. Suddenly the economics correspondents on the news were talking, every night, about trust, confidence – and even faith. The crisis would deepen unless the banks returned to trusting each other. And the public had a role too, it seemed: we had to keep spending rather than cautiously retreat from the marketplace. We had to demonstrate some faith. This entailed trusting the government as it pumped massive sums of money into the banks, to prod them out of their nervous mood.

So the crisis came about because of the banks' misplaced faith: that the dubious financial products they traded would keep on enriching them and the wider economy. And when the crash came the solution was not a new caution, an emphasis on prudent saving, but a determined persistence in capitalist faith, despite the evidence of where such faith led. The natural response was to lambast the reckless faith of the banks, but the experts warned that this response was dangerous, for things would get worse until the banks regained their bullish enthusiasm. So it seemed that the world was in the hands of a reckless elite, and that the most dangerous thing was their suddenly becoming cautious, losing faith.

As the scale of the crisis became clear President Bush gave a speech reminiscent of the one he made after 11 September 2001: he called for a renewed faith in capitalism, as a central pillar of Western values. But what exactly is this faith? And isn't an excess of it the very problem?

Is capitalist faith an offshoot of Christian faith? The clearest evidence of a positive affinity is the parable of the talents (Matthew 25:14–30). A servant is entrusted with some money, and fails to invest it. His master is furious. So Jesus commends the attitude of the risk-taking investor as a model for faith. Does this make Jesus a capitalist? There is no other evidence of Jesus encouraging his disciples to capitalist activity. He does not tell them to start small businesses as signs of the kingdom. And other parables praise the woman who gives her last pennies to charity, and the man who sells all for one beautiful pearl: they are not good capitalists. He also tells a rich young man to give his money away, and warns against the demon Mammon, meaning wealth unhitched to the common good. So all that we can really say is that Jesus, in one instance, uses venture capitalist faith to illustrate what he means by faith in God. But the goodness of capitalist faith depends on the context: in this story it is good because it is in the service of the master (i.e. God).

In early modern times, a new aura of excitement surrounded capitalism, and people began to reflect on the virtue of capitalist faith. Shakespeare's comedy *The Merchant of Venice* is a good example. The merchant, Antonio, wants to fund his young friend's amorous adventure. But all his money is invested in shipping. So he borrows from the moneylender Shylock, confident that he can repay when his ships come in. They don't, and so Shylock gains power over his life. Antonio is the archetypal good capitalist: he puts all his money to work, and he is generous with his wealth. He is imprudently bold, and suicidally generous. And, of course, Shylock is the other side of capitalism: he hoards, and he profits from the cowardly business of usury. It is this separation of duties that allows a virtuous version of capitalism to exist: the romantic, self-giving version of Antonio. What was actually happening at this time was that usury was being legitimized, and so someone like Antonio was able to profit from lending as well as riskier investing.

Modern capitalism always needs to pretend that it is animated by the spirit of Antonio. City bankers set great store on their style, their camaraderie and their generous spending of the money they make – not just because they are hearty hedonists, but also because they want to buy into this image. Perhaps it is not too off the wall to suggest that the banking industry *wants* the system to crash from time to time in order to prove that it is edgy, risky, adventurous, rather than the trough of timid fat cats.

Like Christianity, capitalism is composed of both trust and faith. I *trust* the bank to protect and slightly expand my money and I have *faith* in the start-up company I invest in. The wise investor balances his portfolio between trust and faith options.

Capitalism gained new legitimacy when the Bank of England was founded in 1694, for the state now guaranteed the rising value of capital, creating a bedrock of trust on which increasingly bold ventures of faith could be launched, largely in the new colonies. The new power of money became written into the dominant ideology: liberalism. Economic agency was a key part of the individual's freedom, which the state had to protect. But was this brave new world such a good thing? Didn't it weaken traditional social bonds and unleash greed? Perhaps, wrote Adam Smith in *The Wealth of Nations* in 1776, but it was all for the best: the individual seeking to enrich himself contributes to a general process of enrichment, thanks to the Invisible Hand, by which he means an aspect of divine providence. With this theory, capitalism entails faith in a new sense: it is not just a matter of subjective practical faith that one's investments will flourish; it is also a matter of objective theoretical faith in the goodness of the system. The *general good* is best served by setting people free to get rich; also, of course, it is a matter of liberty that people should be allowed to. In a sense capitalism breathes new life into the old concept of providence.

This free-market "faith" was part of the national ideology since Smith formulated it. But of course it was reined in by other strands: patriotism, liberal Protestantism. It was a sub-faith. It played a huge role in nineteenth-century politics, when it became known as Manchester liberalism. But it was just one strand within the larger liberal ideology of Britain and its empire. During most of the twentieth century it coexisted with socialist reforms, and then the welfare state.

And then, rather suddenly, it was re-born as a faith. Thatcherism gave free-market "neo-liberal" capitalism a prominence it had never had before. This old sub-faith was suddenly a full-blooded faith. Margaret Thatcher was a staunch Methodist in her youth; her adult cause was also a defiant, revivalist faith. This faith was not simply free-market capitalism, but *Britain's moral revival through free-market capitalism.* "Economics are the method", she said in 1981, "the object is to change the heart and soul [of the nation]" (in Gilmour 1992: 128). Once weaned off its semi-socialism, the nation would become morally as well as economically great again, for it would rediscover middle-class responsibility. Her programme consisted of economic dogma, held with moral passion. The intellectual godfather was economist F. A. Hayek, who taught pure faith in the market. Such faith was a radicalization of Smith, with a dose of social Darwinism thrown in. A key aspect was the monetarist theory of American economist Milton Friedman, which most economists were wary of. "But just as Christian fundamentalists remain impervious to modern biblical criticism, the monetarist zealots in the new Conservative government did not allow irksome facts or the existence of different monetarist sects to disturb their faith in the Chicago prophet" (*ibid.*: 16–17). Thatcher was not only a conviction politician but a faith politician. Her genius was to mix this dry economic theory with an earnest nationalism. Her embodiment of this ideology surpassed politics in the normal sense: she produced one of the clearest faith performances in British modern history, at least as iconic as Churchill's in the Second World War. A residually Protestant nation is impressed by such performances. She was a latter-day British Luther, whose most famous utterances, such as "There is no alternative" and "The lady's not for turning" were versions of "Here I stand!"

Owing to this movement, the strongest form of faith in recent British history has been faith in free-market capitalism as a morally regenerative force. As has often been said, this creed was incoherent: the free market is actually corrosive of the traditional bourgeois values she advocated, and a strong centralizing state is needed to clear a path for it. Thatcherism (and Reaganism) was a form of faith: that markets are benign and self-stabilizing, and that their free play is ultimately good for the national soul. But of course this "faith" blurs with something that can hardly be called faith: bourgeois self-interest and greed. It thereby confers an aura of nobility on the latter. It brings a thrilling ambiguity to the phrase "greed is good". So Thatcherism was a fusion of faith (dependent on her iconic faith performance) and pragmatic self-interest, which is the opposite of faith.

The electorate's attraction to this political faith fizzled out. Tony Blair offered a more benign faith: in the general good, in society. But the means was not socialism, but a realistic acceptance of the efficacy of free-market capitalism: it could not re-moralize us, but its neutral power could be harnessed for the general good. He tried to graft a semi-socialist faith on to the free market. This seemed ideal:

socialist idealism, based on the success of neo-liberal capitalism. We should "only connect" the good within capitalism with the good within socialism. His leadership had the same sort of shamanic quality as Thatcher's: what he mainly offered was a performance of faith. For a while his faith in a "new dawn" seemed to infect the nation, but this sense petered out, and the post-socialist idealism seemed to lack substance. The vision was over-reliant on shaman-Blair. His passionate conference-sermons showed the force of his faith, but that faith wasn't really representative of anything wider: he was a pope without a church. In theory, social idealism was *using* neo-liberal economics, in a cunning looting of the Egyptians; but it began to seem that the "looted" ideology was actually in the driving seat. Britain's politics might have been mildly socialist, but its *culture* continued in the opposite direction, with crass hedonism becoming further normalized. Blair should have said that culture, as well as fiscal policy, must change if we are to rediscover the idea of society. What the New Labour years have shown is that neo-liberal capitalism is stronger than any other political faith, despite being not very popular. Even when a left-wing party is given a strong mandate it cannot really supplant it. The attempt to subordinate it to socialist idealism fails, for it asserts itself as truer, more culturally rooted, than the idealism laid on top of it.

Has the current crash shaken our default ideology? Up to a point. The idea of fully free markets, the Washington consensus, has been clearly exposed as a false faith, and unprecedented plans are underway for the regulation of international finance. And there is a new wave of scepticism about the wider faith, that the wealth of a super-rich elite will trickle down, that there is no alternative to extreme inequality. But once the storm has passed, won't the old faith reassert itself, in the absence of any other? Perhaps so, but it has been put in doubt like never before, not just by the crash, but also by another, more permanent storm brewing, another shaking force at work. It has become impossible to ignore the fact that economic growth threatens the planet. We have a new reason to dislike our default political faith, diluted Thatcherism. But can environmentalism bring a new sort of political faith?

In his book *Capitalism and Religion* (2002), Philip Goodchild asks how we can tame this system – globalized capitalism – that is hurling us towards disaster. The problem is that no political, moral or religious system can claim to be as universally true as economic rationality. Having ideas about human well-being is all very nice, but the truth of the marketplace is always truer. This was Marx's key insight: that in capitalism money becomes the arbiter of objective value. He thought that this bad universalism could only be trumped by the good universalism of proletarian revolution. But history has proved him wrong: "revolution" lacks this sort of final purity. So what can trump the dark objectivity of money-value? Only the prospect of apocalypse, says Goodchild. This possible event really does concern everyone, absolutely. Capitalism has "led to the true universal of ecological limits. In order to survive we require a new universal form of reason" (2002: 252). Goodchild suggests that only the fear of apocalypse can really outdo the universalism of capitalism.

At present it seems that such thinking is seeping into the mainstream. For a decade or so the "anti-globalization" protesters have seemed risibly vague: what nice new order do they want, instead of nasty capitalism? But now many commentators accept that the question is urgent, even if the answer is unclear.

If only the prospect of apocalypse can challenge capitalism, maybe a new sort of faith will take centre stage. The flipside of apocalypse is the utopian ideal of uniting humanity and saving the planet. Capitalism must be made subservient to an ideal of the well-being of the planet and all humanity.

But how can it be? A nicer version of capitalism sounds like a nicer version of the sexual appetite, free of irresponsible lust. How can this naive-sounding idealism affect actual politics? Maybe the only thing that can save us is the advent of a new faith – one that would recently have been dismissed as utopian folly.

Psychology: what is normal?

Well, the reader might be saying, maybe we always need a sort of faith in our political leaders, and yes, we must beware the quasi-faith of turbo-capitalism, but aren't these secondary forms of faith? Isn't real, full-scale faith more personal than that? In this section I want to ask: does a secular version of faith play a role in psychology?

Psychological health clearly involves trust: unless one is reasonably trusting of strangers, one falls into paranoia. Similarly, it entails a certain amount of optimism: so we can talk of trust and optimism as features of psychological health, but what about *faith*? As we saw in the introduction, faith is stronger than trust, more dramatic, dynamic, defiant. Can we claim that faith belongs to psychological health?

I want to suggest that psychological health entails at least an *echo* of religious faith. Here is a little example of the echo. The word "despair" is still sometimes used for intense depression: if someone seems acutely unhappy we might say that he is "in despair". There is an implication here that the healthy person needs the opposite of despair: hope, or faith. But why should he or she need it?

The strange thing about psychology is that it struggles to speak about the normal state. What is the psychological state of the normal, healthy person? Happiness? Stable satisfaction? Fully successful selfhood? I think most people would flinch from such answers (and perhaps emit a hollow laugh). We all have issues, it might be said: there's always something to get you down. That doesn't mean we're miserable. As mothers are advised to eschew perfection and settle for being "good enough", most of us can claim to be "happy enough". Well, that is probably what most of us would say if quizzed on the matter. But it hardly tells the whole story. It hardly does justice to those moods (are they passing moods or most-of-the-time moods?) when it all looks rather bleak and we struggle to imagine how we'll get by. Depression? Or is that something more serious? It's hard to say. We surely don't look in bafflement at people who suffer from depression.

So maybe one could describe psychological normality as being happy enough but acquainted with the case for depression, or perhaps as being aware of the threat of depression. How menacing is this threat? Surely most people are sufficiently aware of it to have developed certain half-conscious strategies for warding it off. This is a basic part of one's interior dialogue. No, the glass is *not* half empty but half full.

If it is normal to experience the threat of depression, and to respond by trying to be positive, then an effort of psychological positiveness is a very basic part of selfhood, and of course this effort is faith-territory. In which case, why is our culture more or less silent on this? Why do we have almost no language for this phenomenon, no shared way of acknowledging it?

Am I overstating it, to suggest that it is normal to contend with a depressive perspective? Much depends on what we mean by "depression". The problem is that depression only really gets talked about when it is something for which people seek professional treatment. These sufferers seem to be more *really* depressed than those who simply cope with it, considering it to be part of their psychological make-up. Maybe there are two forms: a stronger form that drives people to seek help, and a milder form that people manage to cope with. On the other hand, maybe not. The same level of depression might afflict two people; one seeks treatment, the other does not. The first person's depression becomes official, serious, and the second person's remains hidden. This would confirm the process by which we link depression, or "real depression", or "clinical depression", with that which seeks professional treatment. The condition becomes pathologized. Depression that is quietly borne is not something that really registers in public discourse, at least not in a direct, explicit way. Owing to the current prevalence of testimonies of extreme depression, the normal person feels reluctant to identify his or her "mild" depression as depression. This is partly out of fear of stigma: if depression is a form of mental illness, then I had better not admit to my periodic feelings of strong gloom. And it is partly out of a sort of humility: I am not pretending that my sufferings are as serious as that poor person's. (With celebrities it is different: depression becomes a source of the specialness that is one's livelihood.) So the more depression is spoken of as a serious business, the more a divide opens up between Serious Depression, and the normal person's experience of feeling gloomy. When a celebrity talks of his struggle with clinical depression, in an attempt to "lift the taboo" surrounding mental illness, the effort is strangely counterproductive. It strengthens the assumption that psychological normality is depressionless, that healthy people do not have to struggle with this except an unfortunate few (some of whom manage to spin themselves as special). It therefore makes the majority *less* willing to admit to depressive feelings, less able to see it as normal.

In my opinion it is a massively important part of secular modernity that we pathologize disaffection: see it as something in need of a cure, rather than as a normal human state. The problem is that a culture cannot remain neutral on the question of whether it is normal to know depression, angst, spiritual (i.e. psychological) disaffection. Unless it says this is normal, and upholds a narrative accounting for its normality, then it implies it is abnormal. This is what our culture does: it encourages the assumption that the human psyche is naturally all right, as the human body is. What is wrong with this assumption? It misleads us about the achievability of happiness, psychological peace. Happiness ought to come naturally, it says; you ought to be free of psychological unease just as you ought to be free of physical disease. This makes it hard for us to cope with the reality: that the human psyche struggles to be happy-enough. It magnifies the threat of negativity, for the normal occurrence of contending with gloom is not seen as normal but as borderline mental illness.

On one level this sketch of secular psychology, as the assumption of natural happiness, is a simplistic caricature: no serious adult thinks it is like this. But what *is* it like, according to these serious adults? There is no alternative secular narrative about the human psyche, so the crude one dominates (helped along by the advertising industry). Normal is happy; struggling to be happy-enough is disaffected, ill.

How do we cope? Increasingly badly, according to mental health statistics. But how do we cope at all? By letting the truth slip out. It can't be voiced in normal secular discourse, for it is too close to an admission of abnormality. So we rely heavily on the arts, and the gossip industry. Instead of admitting that it is normal to experience psychological struggle, we gawp at the troubled lives of suicidal artists, such as Sylvia Plath, which is essentially a highbrow version of reading about Diana or Britney. Our intense interest in the psychological car crashes of celebrities, and artists, is due to the lack of a common discourse about psychological struggle. We need to elevate these figures, in a ritualistic way. We need to read endless stories about how footballers are "battling with their demons" because we cannot quite admit that *we* are battling with *our* demons. Secular culture doesn't allow us to see our own inner drama as normal, so we latch on to extreme and gaudy versions of it: public spectacles of inner angst. Pop music is also crucial here. It is a space in which angst can be aired: songs about unhappy love are really also about the lonely struggle of selfhood. The disco anthem "I Will Survive" is ostensibly about getting over a relationship, but is also about existential resolution and defiance (also known as faith).

Tracing the origins of the modern psychological paradigm is beyond our scope, but let's venture a brief word. The religious revolution of the sixteenth century undermined a stable account of religious selfhood. Throughout Christendom, it had been assumed that the psyche needed God, to complete it, stabilize it. On its own, it was prey to demonic forces. In Elizabethan times, we see the new, autonomous selves of Doctor Faustus, of Hamlet. But this is ambiguous: for look what torment they are in. Maybe the old model of selfhood – we're lost without God – remains true, but the idea was emerging that psychological unease was abnormal, that the healthy person was naturally free of it. This is the implication behind Robert Burton's fat book *The Anatomy of Melancholy* (1621). So a tension arose between the old religious view, and the new secular view, as the psychologist Darian Leader has recently noted:

> Historically, the distinction between a natural and an unnatural melancholia had often been unclear: to what extent was a certain melancholia a part of human existence and to what extent was it an illness that needed to be treated? How could one distinguish between melancholic despair and that induced by a "true" sense of sin? (2008: 34)

Through seeking to understand and alleviate acute mental angst, this new discourse implies the non-necessity of all angst. For a century or so, the new secular paradigm was waiting in the wings: the intense religiosity of someone like the seventeenth-century author of *The Pilgrim's Progress* John Bunyan remained semi-normal. In the early eighteenth century it moved centre stage, as historian Roy Porter explains:

> In traditional charts of knowledge, the study of the mind or soul had fallen under the heading of "pneumatology" ... within the domain of divinity. Enlightened discourse, by contrast, began to map out a field of natural knowledge pertaining to the mind which was distinct from the theological study of the immortal soul. Thus *Chambers Cyclopaedia* (1727) defined psychology as "a Discourse Concerning the Soul" which

constituted a part not of theology but rather of anthropology,
that is, the natural study of man at large.   (2000: 170)

The idea crept in that the soul could be rationally understood –
and so did the idea that the soul was, like the body, naturally healthy.
The essence of health was the pursuit of rational self-interest, or
happiness. The ideal of the age was the man "whose moderate
pursuit of rational pleasures in social settings would produce
lasting enjoyment ... Enlightened thought thus gave its blessing
to the pursuit of pleasure ... [it] promoted refined hedonism and
enlightened self-interest within consumer capitalism" (*ibid.*: 265).
A normal psyche is disposed to happy capitalist activity: away with
the gloomy medievalism that doubts it!

This ideology has steadily chipped away at the old religious view
of selfhood, and since the 1960s it has dominated more easily than
ever. The result is that our culture can only give oblique expression to the central matter of psychology: that we struggle against
pessimism, that we need faith. For there is no overarching narrative of such struggle. The overarching narrative is: healthy is happy.
Of course this is a problem for religion, to put it mildly. Religion
presupposes that we need to be "saved", which means that it presupposes that we are naturally in a bad way, we need putting right;
the individual soul is troublesome, unstable, prone to despair. The
essential secular response to this is to say, "We're fine, thanks. The
psychological unease that you call normal? We call that neurotic".
How can the religious point of view respond to this? It's not easy,
for it seems to be calling black white, when it calls psychological
health deficient. It sounds unbelievably gloomy, to want to rede-
scribe normality in this negative way; it sounds like a dark form
of neurosis, that wants to spread itself through society, become
"normal". What the religious point of view must do, in the face of
the "healthy is happy" myth, is to unsettle, deconstruct; it must
point to the places where honesty leaks out.

Literature is such a place. One of the most important English poets of the second half of the twentieth century was Philip Larkin; no other poetic voice became so widely and deeply known. His appeal was that he expressed the side of psychology that secular modernity shuns. Normality, he said, is gloomier than mainstream culture is willing to admit. Do we therefore need faith, to get us through? He rejected religious faith, but he certainly had a sort of faith in poetry, as if seeing life clearly was a sort of calling, and he also valued a very English form of stoicism: mustn't make a fuss (for a fuller account of this see my recent essay on his quasi-religious self-understanding; Hobson 2006). Of course he is often called a gloomy old git, a depressive, but his popularity, and literary stature, makes it harder to dismiss him as such. It would be strange to say, "his poetry is pretty irrelevant because he was clearly depressed, and most of us aren't". Instead, his popularity exposes the falsity of pathologizing depression; it suggests that there is more univer- sality here than ordinary discourse is able to admit. Larkin was consciously attacking the complacent, evasive psychology of modernity. He once said that the novels he valued most highly were about the mundane struggles of ordinary people, showing "a real- istic firmness & even humour", and "a rueful yet courageous accept- ance of things which I think more relevant to life as most of us have to live it than spies coming in from the cold" (Larkin 1992: 376). His own poetry attempts to show these qualities under the guise of half- ironic despair. It re-describes ordinary selfhood as a hard struggle: to be happy enough, to behave decently enough.

This is really a continuation of Romanticism, which was (partly) a reaction against the secular idea of progress, the secularization of psychology that we have noted. The poetry that William Wordsworth wrote at the end of the eighteenth century was a revival of essen- tially religious psychology: the poet is a sensitive soul who struggles against depression, who pioneers a new sort of *faith*. Like Larkin, but more positively, he was giving voice to the experience of inner struggle that modern rationality was subtly marginalizing. Actually, he says, the most basic reality is not industrial progress, or even political revolution (he had cheered on the French Revolution, then had his hopes dashed), but one's sense of awe, of aloneness, of yearning: the drama of being a suffering, striving soul. In 1799 he wrote the first draft of his long autobiographical poem *The Prelude*. The climax explains that natural beauty is the source of this new faith:

> ... if, in this time
> Of dereliction and dismay, I yet
> Despair not of our nature, but retain
> A more than Roman confidence, a faith
> That fails not, in all sorrow my support,
> The blessing of my life, the gift is yours,
> Ye mountains, thine, O Nature.

He inherits the neo-classical idea that nature, in a wide sense, is to be trusted – and radicalizes it. A comfy trust is not enough: we need a defiant faith. "A more than Roman confidence" sounds like Christian faith. What we need is not just a vague trust in social progress; we need something that is fully soul-involving, a new secular version of *Christian faith*. His poetry performs this new faith, and it only really makes sense if one shares his presupposition that *we need saving* – from the oppressive difficulty of ordinary modern life. As he puts it in "Lines Composed a Few Miles Above Tintern Abbey", Nature will protect us, she will see that no depressing reality

> Shall e'er prevail against us, or disturb
> Our chearful faith that all which we behold
> Is full of blessings ...

The rhetoric of conflict ("prevail") is reminiscent of St Paul. We need faith that the world is good, despite the angst of daily life.

We need this faith in order to feel positive about our lives and to feel grateful for creation. The condition that religion presupposed remains: the soul is in need of assurance; it is not already all right.

So the key question relating to psychology in a secular age is this: do we need saving? No, is the official reply: that concept has been left behind; the old idea that we are needy sinners, naturally in despair, has been cleared out. We're naturally all right. But the cultural respect paid to poets such as Wordsworth and Larkin tells another story: we value the honesty of those who dissent from this by relating their gravitation to despair, and their need to be delivered from it, by some new version of faith.

At the risk of sounding a touch polemical, the whole modern discourse of psychology has been amazingly, shamefully weak. It has been subservient to the ideology of the naturally happy consumer. Perhaps this is inevitable: in the absence of a narrative of the psyche's normal disaffection, disaffection will be pathologized. Medical and psychiatric experts cannot help backing this up: their study of the acutely disaffected will naturally posit a divide between health and ill health, which confirms the cultural narrative.

Was the founder of psychoanalysis Sigmund Freud any wiser? He approached secular psychology with a sort of prophetic gravitas. He said that it is normal to live in a state of inner struggle, whose root cause is the necessary repression of sexuality. We all have to suffer the discontents that civilized behaviour brings. Those who become neurotic are those who have a fault in their machinery of repression, but we are all low-level neurotics, for there is no perfect working of this awesome, brutal machinery. On one level he introduces healthy realism to psychology; he attacks the "healthy is happy" assumption by pointing to a sort of structural flaw in us. Yet in doing so, he is hugely over-prescriptive about the nature of psychological struggle. It *must* be understood in relation to the after-effects of infantile sexuality! Because this master theory received such attention, and now seems absurdly dogmatic, it did damage to the idea of inner struggle, what might be called realistic psychology. It made it easier to dismiss. (In the same way, Marxism did damage to the idea of social hope. More of that later.)

In recent decades, ordinary unhappiness has been pathologized to an extent that was previously imagined only by Aldous Huxley in his novel *Brave New World*. Or, rather, it has been medicalized: antidepressants have become part of the cultural landscape – the literal opiate of the masses. But there are a few signs that psychology is waking up to its fundamental failure: its failure to help people to cope with normality.

The psychologist Oliver James has been trying to dissuade people from expecting effortless happiness, warning that this leads to depressive disappointment. He attacks the idea that we can become happy through having enough stuff, which he calls "affluenza". What is relevant to our purposes is that James sees a large part of the solution to this as a move away from happiness as the ideal. "I regard happiness as chimeric and temporary, akin to pleasure, and I tend to agree with the saying, 'We are not put on this earth to be happy'" (2007: xiv). Instead we must cultivate the virtue of optimism, he says. He explains that he does not mean the shallow "positive thinking" that dominates parts of American culture: the thing that writer and social activist Barbara Ehrenreich (2008) blames for the financial crisis. He means a form of optimism that does not hide away from the negative side of life, but takes it for granted, and learns to affirm life in spite of it. This entails blurring the line between normality and the experience of depression. He avoids the word, for fear of seeming to have a religious agenda, but he is talking about faith: our society is sick for the lack of it, for the lack of a public acknowledgement of its necessity.

This section has been absurdly wide-ranging: its aim was to raise the question of whether psychological health might have more room for the concept of faith than secular psychology admits.

3. After Abraham

We have seen that the concept of faith relates to some of the most important debates of our day. Democratic politics is not just a matter of the endless detail of policy decisions. There is also "the vision thing", and the concept of faith has a starring role here. The electorate is hungry to put its faith in a leader who is not just a competent manager, and decent enough; he should also seem to have faith in the future. If his faith is sufficiently strong, we seem to feel, then he might be able to foster a whole new era of belief in the common good. Maybe believing in the common good is so hard that we need an inspiring exemplar, to guide us. And we must also refer to faith when thinking through the crisis of global capitalism. Has capitalism been too faith based? Have we dangerously idealized the role of risk, and made money-making too ideologically sexy? How can we dampen this down, and try to convert faith in the markets to faith in the general good? Faith also plays a role, albeit a background one, in the discourse of psychological health. Why has disaffection grown, in a time of affluence? Do we have a collective attitude problem, rooted in an expectation that happiness is a natural right? Can we recover something of the old religious understanding of the psyche, as a naturally problematic entity that can be redeemed by adopting the right attitude – of radical positivity?

If our political and personal well-being is to some degree faith based, then enquiry into the meaning of faith is not as marginal a matter as some might assume. As I suggested in the introduction, faith differs from its near-synonyms hope and trust in retaining a stronger religious link, in being harder to secularize. To understand why, we need to sketch the role of faith in Judaeo-Christian tradition.

Around the ninth century BCE, a couple of centuries after settling in their allegedly promised land, the Jewish people started writing down their myths. They looked back on the tall stories of their migration to this land. They traced their origins to a particular tribal leader, Abraham. And they also recorded a pre-history: God's creation of the world, and his dealings with the very first human beings. The main author of the first books of the Bible is known as J. This writer, more than anyone else, is responsible for inventing the concept of faith. For when these ancient stories were written down, the theme of faith was given prominence. Whether this theme had always been emphasized, in the centuries of oral telling, we cannot know. But now it was – and this literary and religious decision changed the world.

The first hero of faith in the Bible is Noah (Genesis 6–9). He finds favour with God by being morally upright in contrast to everyone else. God tells him to build a massive boat and fill it with animals. He obeys. We are not told what his neighbours thought about his action, but his sanity was presumably questioned. This is our first sketch of faith: Noah's decision to listen to God's unlikely instructions, to take a totally singular course of action. His faith is rewarded: not only does God allow him to survive the flood and to prosper afterwards, but he also makes a deal with him. He promises never again to wipe out the world with a flood. Noah's obedience has won him an assurance that from now on creation will cohere.

Soon we hear of a man called Abram, who lives in the Babylonian city of Ur. God tells him to emigrate, to leave his native land for a new one that will be shown to him, to become the founder of a new people. He obeys the call (Genesis 12). Faith and obedience are of course very closely linked. (Islam is particularly keen on the theme of obedience, or submission – indeed "Islam" means "submission".)

We are given no psychological detail, but it seems unnecessary to spell out that his decision is risky, half-mad, unnatural. "Throughout the entire story one must always remember that to leave home and to break ancestral bonds was to expect of ancient man almost the impossible", says the biblical scholar Gerhardt von Rad (1961: 161). We are not told that he is particularly virtuous, and his first adventure suggests otherwise. He goes to Egypt and seemingly pimps his wife to Pharaoh, saying she's his sister. He seems like a hard, cunning, pioneer type. When God reappears to him, Abram reminds him that he is childless. Relax, says God, you will father a great people, as numerous as the stars in the sky. "Abram believed the Lord, and he credited it to him as righteousness" (Genesis 15:6). This is his claim to righteousness: trusting this vision. It is important to note that God has not yet given him any instructions concerning morality or ritual. This was to be hugely important to the founder of Christianity, Paul. What made him pleasing to God was not anything he did, but the simple fact that he trusted him.

In a further vision, God announces a covenant with this tribe, whose outward mark is circumcision. He also tells Abram to change his name to Abraham. And he tells him that his wife will conceive, although she is past childbearing age (Genesis 17). His faith is thus rewarded with miraculous fecundity (this link between faith and fertility is crucial to the Bible). So his wife bears a son, Isaac, and soon the grim story of the near-sacrifice is told. God tells him, "Take your son, your only son Isaac, whom you love, and go to the region of Moriah. Sacrifice him there as a burnt offering on one of the mountains I will tell you about". He prepares to do so (Genesis 22). We are told nothing of his state of mind; we are left to infer it from the fact that he loves his son. He seems unfeeling, cold, even psychopathic, for we are only told about his businesslike actions, his saddling of the donkey, his gathering of wood for the immolation. God provides alternative meat at the last minute, just as he has raised the knife against his son, and tells him, "because you have done this and have not withheld your son, your only son, I will surely bless you and make your descendants as numerous as the stars in the sky and as the sand on the seashore". Why does God arrange this grim test? Hasn't Abraham long since proved his obedience, by leaving his native city? He has to demonstrate his awareness that his blessings are from God, not his own doing. He has to acknowledge that Isaac came to him by God's miracle, and so he does not own him.

After Abraham's death, God reveals himself to Isaac, and then to Isaac's son Jacob. Jacob is cunning and stubborn. At one point God appears to him in the form of a man who engages him in a wrestling match: Jacob gives as good as he gets (Genesis 32). This seems to suggest that faith is not a matter of smooth pious obedience but a state of fight: with oneself, the world and even God.

So far it is the charismatic tribal leader who is given the divine vision. A clash between worldly and religious authority is thus avoided. This changes with Jacob's son Joseph, who seems to receive divine visions by means of dreams. But these visions are of his own future greatness, so there is good reason to dismiss him as a spoiled brat. His father advises him to keep quiet (Genesis 37). Here is the Bible's first hint that faith is problematic, akin to antisocial arrogance. Why should someone who claims to receive divine visions be believed? Isn't the claim probably just a bid for power, for personal glory? Yet the point of the Joseph story is that God does reveal himself through this cocky youngster. His arrogance is justified. Even though it is socially disruptive, God vindicates it, makes use of it. Joseph's travails give us a first glimpse of the suffering prophet figure, yet he is mainly the plucky hero of an exotic adventure story. And the problem of religious and worldly authority conflicting is overcome when he finds fame and fortune in Egypt, and becomes the effective tribal leader. The story shows God's capacity to reverse adversity: what looks like injustice and misfortune becomes the means to the tribe's salvation. Faith in God's plan is always warranted.

The Moses story is the turning point of the Old Testament. Before Moses, this religious tradition was frail and unpredictable, dangerously dependent on individuals' claim to visionary experience. Of course, Moses has another visionary experience, but it leads towards the regularization of the religion. He is the heroic tribal leader, the liberator, who brings new objectivity to this God. The vision becomes fixed, objective, rule based. The covenant is no longer a private arrangement between God and the tribal leader; it is something that the entire Jewish people is expected to be aware of, and committed to.

Moses's interview with God is far more fleshed out than its precedents. We are told of his surprise, his fear and, when he hears God's plan, his self-doubt (Exodus 3). Will he be able to convince his fellow Israelites that his calling is real? Who should he say is calling? He even tries to back out completely: "O Lord, please send someone else to do it" (Exodus 4:13). It seems that the ordinary person is supposed to identify with Moses, to feel psychologically related to this hero of faith.

The Exodus story brings new substance to God. He is not just a voice who issues a vague promise that this tribe will prosper. He is an actual military force to be reckoned with. But the Israelites quickly forget this: on their journey through the wilderness they start grumbling about food and water shortages, failing to understand that God will miraculously provide what is needed. This is the first characterization of Israel as a collective person, struggling to trust God's leadership. At Mount Sinai, Moses is told to mediate God's promise to the whole nation, that they are specially favoured (Exodus 19:4). The Ten Commandments begin with the commandment that God must be exclusively trusted. To acknowledge his authority is to agree that no rival deity should be honoured, for he is "a jealous God". There follows a long series of laws, which in practice evolved in subsequent centuries, but are ascribed to Moses to heighten their authority. God provides rules about worship, and instructions for the self-assembly of a mobile sanctuary. In other words, God suddenly organizes a religion for his people.

Where does this leave the concept of faith? Once an organized religion is in place, the heroic faith of Abraham, Jacob, Joseph and Moses becomes ambiguous. It is of course exemplary: all Jews should display such absolute trust in God. Yet to see it as a direct example is dangerous. It would lead to many subversive claims to visionary authority. After Moses, the idea is that all of Israel is a corporate person, with the faith that was modelled by the founders. The individual does not imitate Abraham: he participates in the nation's imitation of Abraham. And organized religion enables this participation; indeed, because God's laws cover all aspects of life, all of cultural life is "organized religion", and it is all based on the signifying of trust.

So the Old Testament charts a major transition from the absolute freedom of Abraham's faith-vision, to the laws of Exodus and Leviticus. The idea that God's will can be communicated directly to a special individual gives way to the idea that his will is expressed in cultural rules. But the former side of faith does not disappear; it is firmly within the DNA of this religious culture, and so it resurfaces. Once the promised land is settled, and Israel opts to become a monarchy, we hear of people called prophets; they seem to have formed a counter-cultural movement, which the first king, Saul, had to keep onside. They criticized Israel's habit of imitating other kingdoms, importing their religious and cultural habits. This tradition continued in the eighth century BCE, with the first prophets whose actual words were lengthily recorded. Amos and Hosea lambasted the pagan drift, and recorded their own experience of being called by God to speak out. The key message was that God's plan for Israel still stood, despite Israel's breaking of the covenant. This message was reasserted by Isaiah: if Israel returns to the straight and narrow, a new era of peace is possible. A truly great leader will emerge, finally solving all the grim problems of political life. Is this a secular histor- ical hope or a supernatural one? It seems to veer from the former to the latter. The thought of a righteous political saviour veers off into utopian imagery about the wolf and the lamb becoming friends, and God's will being done throughout the world. But first there must be judgement, disaster: there is no immediate route to this utopian vision, but it is God's ultimate plan for Israel – and for all the nations. According to Jeremiah, God will ultimately recreate humanity, giving us new hearts that are naturally good. His law will not be such a struggle to obey, for he will write it on our hearts. They were right about the calamity: Israel collapsed, and was largely preserved in exile, in Babylon, during the sixth century BCE. The exile provoked new, defiant expressions of faith. Despite appearances, God still planned to restore Israel, and use it to save the world.

These prophetic writings deepen the concept of faith. The prophet is a dramatically disaffected figure: ill at ease in the extreme. He can't deal with the idea that some of his compatriots are comfortably off while others are starving. He refuses to accept this as reality. The true reality is that a new era of absolute peace is possible. Of course, this follows the tradition of God's promise to Abraham. Because God has chosen us, we are not meant to be a normal nation, full of violence and insecurity: we are destined to become the perfectly peaceful human society – and the wider world will learn from us.

With the exile, it becomes increasingly important for Israel to trust that God has a plan, despite the evidence. The Psalms reflect this. Although many of them predate the exile, the collection is coloured by this concern, known as "theodicy": how can God allow bad things to happen? The Psalms are songs that seem to have been sung by shaman figures, as part of worship. In many cases, the speaker tells of terrible suffering, of being victimized, of feeling shamefully weak, and struggles to affirm God's plan even from within this predicament. It is recalled that God created and sustains all things, and so he should be trusted to end present travails and put everything right. Bad people who trust in themselves and mock God's law will get their comeuppance. The Psalms are snapshots of an individual's struggle to have faith in God, but they fulfilled a social function. This very personal drama is the key totem of the group identity, and the key theme of worship. This paradox is central to the Jewish faith. The collective imagines itself as a corporate individual, a lonely victim who yearns for God's rule.

So it seems that Jewish religion becomes increasingly focused on this dynamic: God is to be trusted despite his seeming abandonment of his people. This is a strange form for a religion to take. Can a religion really function if a sense of abandonment, of crisis, is so central to it? There is a danger that this theme of suffering will become hackneyed, inauthentic. If you congregate to sing songs of suffering, isn't there a danger that the pathos will become stale, that you'll be faking it? The Book of Job seems to be a reflection on this danger. Like the speaker of the Psalms, Job struggles to trust God, despite his suffering. The genius of this book is to make this dynamic fresh, by rejecting it as an orthodoxy, a formula. It has to be an insight that is personally achieved, suffered for. So Job rejects the teaching of his friends that God must be trusted, even in suffering. No, says Job, this is a stale orthodoxy. I want to put my case to God directly, and get a personal answer. He is accused of arrogance, for thinking his suffering so unique that it merits an explanation from God. Yet God grants him a one-to-one, in which he announces his majestic providence. The book's message seems to be that this theme, of faith in the midst of suffering, cannot be allowed to become routine, an ideology, a creed: it must be reasserted with passionate freshness. The individual is right to see his own experience of it as absolutely important – it can never become a piece of group-think. This existential drama is the essence of this religion: don't let institutional experts normalize it, ossify it.

But how can a religion focused on crisis and suffering also be a stable social ideology? Alongside the high-energy faith dramas of the prophets, Israel had a gentler, more reasonable idea of God, known as the wisdom tradition. Here the believer needs no leap of faith in which a supra-historical reversal is envisaged. Instead, he needs only remember that God is on the side of reason, order, the laws of nature as well of revelation. The main expression of this tradition is the Book of Proverbs, but many of the Psalms reflect it too. One relates to God in a rational way: through knowledge, understanding. His "law" is often spoken of, but it is not seen as miraculously revealed to Moses, but as a sort of higher common sense (specific cultic laws are ignored). Wisdom is the divine principle, by which God created the world: it is built into the structure of reality. We human beings need to learn this principle, be taught it as "law": it chiefly consists of charitable action, sexual restraint and avoidance of pride. Wisdom is a faith-based science. Those who behave badly are ignorant: fools. (There is an echo of the Greek equation of goodness with knowledge.) This account of faith is therefore completely at odds with the modern assumption that faith is opposed to reason. It is awareness of the real structure of the universe, which is charity-shaped, God-shaped. There is in the Bible no concept of non-religious rationality that questions this: the person who denies God is the selfish hedonist, not the sceptical philosopher.

Of course, this gently reasonable account of faith overlaps with the more agonistic, dramatic, counter-rational one. The two complement each other. To put it another way, ancient Judaism dodges the question of whether faith, or God-trust, entails a defiance of rationality. Its stories imply yes, but its wisdom teaching says no.

At the end of the Old Testament period, the dramatic and seemingly irrational account of faith comes to the fore in texts known as apocalyptic. The author of the Book of Daniel imagines a sudden supernatural reversal that will institute God's rule. As we saw, the previous prophets were primarily focused on history coming right, and Israel becoming a beacon of peace. This hope is still present, but it coexists with another sort of hope: the resurrection of the dead. Previously, the Jews seem not to have had much sense of an individual afterlife; their focus was more social and historical. But now the idea developed that the dead would be raised at the end of history. This is obviously another form of theodicy: how can God allow innocents to be slaughtered in war? It must be that they will come back, on a day of restitution and judgement. And the traditional idea of a great new ruler who would save Israel becomes tied up with this apocalyptic tradition, so that a supernatural messiah figure seems to be expected, at least by some Jews. A cosmic conflict between good and evil will occur, and God's power will finally be fully revealed.

Our brief survey of Old Testament faith has shown its flexibility. It is on the one hand a dramatically counter-rational form of individualism, and on the other a reasonable social thing. What is clear is that no one ever worries about the question of whether or not God exists. Literary theorist Terry Eagleton makes the point well:

> For most people today, including a lot of religious believers, [the question, "Do you believe in God?"] is unconsciously modelled on questions like "Do you believe in Father Christmas?", or "Do you believe in alien abductions?" On this view, there are certain beings, all the way from God and the Yeti to the Loch Ness Monster and the crew of UFOs, who may or may not exist. The evidence is equivocal, and opinion is accordingly divided on the matter. But an ancient Hebrew would probably not have imagined that "Do you believe in God?" meant anything like that. Since the presence of Yahweh was proclaimed by the whole earth and heavens, the question could only mean: "Do you have faith in him?" It was a matter of a practice, not of an intellectual proposition. It asked about a relationship, not about an opinion.   (2007: 26)

Slovenian philosopher Slavoj Žižek makes the same sort of point: "Apropos of the ancient Jews, they BELIEVED IN many gods and spirits, but what Jehovah demanded from them was to HAVE FAITH only in Him, to respect the symbolic pact between the Jewish people and their God who has chosen them" (2001: 109).

Christianity is the development of certain strands within this complex tradition. In Mark's Gospel especially, Jesus is an energetic prophet and exorcist, and an eccentric student of the Jewish law. Like the prophets he announces a dramatic new thing, a new dawn: the kingdom of God. But he suggests that it is starting *now*. His healing and teaching should be seen as a series of signs that it has begun; he is a sort of performance artist. He talks about Satan a lot. His teaching and behaviour are dominated by a spirit of impish fecundity and enthusiasm. "Get up", he tells the cripple; "Follow me", he tells the taxman; "Why shouldn't I pick corn?", he asks the Pharisee; "Let's eat", he tells a crowd (Mark 2–6). And his stories are about fecundity: the sowing of corn; a mustard seed becoming a massive tree. For a while he sounds like a manic seed merchant. One of his first parables simply tells of a man who sows some seed and is amazed by the plentiful crop that springs up. That's all that happens. Jesus is giving his hearers a little image of natural success, of life really working. Let human life be like this, is the message. Soon he is out on a boat with his followers, and quells a storm. His friends remain scared. "Why are you so afraid? Do you still have no faith?" he asks them (Mark 4:41). (Recall that the Greek word for faith, "*pistis*", which is a translation of the Hebrew "*emunah*", could equally be rendered "trust".) Soon Jesus shows calmness in the face of a self-harming madman. Then he is surrounded by a throng, and a woman takes the liberty of healing herself by touching him, or rather just his clothes. He asks who it was and tells the woman, "Daughter, your faith has healed you" (Mark 5:34). What is "faith" in this context? A belief that Jesus can work miracles, but also a more general trust in God, which seems also to be a trust in goodness and health.

Jesus manifests an attitude of extreme confidence, and requires this attitude from his followers. When he sends out his disciples to spread his message, he tells them to be unprepared, in practical terms; instead of taking food and money they should trust that God will provide (Mark 6:8). This assault on anxiety extends to food rules; people shouldn't worry about becoming polluted by things they eat.

The father of a possessed boy asks for his help.

"If you can do anything, take pity on us and help us."

"If you can?" said Jesus. "Everything is possible for him who believes" (Mark 8:22–3).

Soon he seemingly tells the disciples that it's impossible for rich people to be saved, and then appears to reverse the verdict: "With man this is impossible, but not with God; all things are possible with God" (Mark 10:27). This phrase could sum up most of his teaching. The last parable told by Jesus in Mark's account is of the widow who puts her only penny in the collection: give all, don't be cautious (Mark 12:42–4).

Luke's Gospel begins with the calling of Mary, "the Annunciation": her faith in God's miraculous plan for her is reminiscent of Abraham and his wife, and her song of praise is very like a psalm. In Catholic tradition especially, her faith is a key model for the Christian. According to Archbishop of Canterbury Rowan Williams:

> It's quite hard to imagine the depth and the level and the cost of what is asked of her by God in Luke's story of the Annunciation; to look at her and to meditate on her "yes" and seek her friendship in prayer is not at all an eccentric or foolish thing for a Christian to do if we are to grow in trust.   (2007: 77)

A more Protestant writer would say: we must imitate that faith; Catholic tradition presents her faith as a sort of icon, which helps us to *trust* God.

In Luke as in Mark, a major part of Jesus' teaching is an attitude of trusting expectation. The prayer he teaches his disciples includes the confident command "Give us this day our daily bread". Jesus then expands on this: you have to be persistent in asking God for what you need. It's as if you need something from your neighbour but he's keen to stay in bed rather than help: keep on at him and he'll get up to get rid of you. This is a strange picture of God! He modifies this with another image: if you're a father with a son pestering to be fed, of course you'll satisfy him (Luke 11). (I often think of this passage when my children are pestering me for snacks or drinks). So he is teaching an attitude of deep confidence: assume that your flourishing is possible, natural, what God plans. Experience might seem to contradict this, but this is a superficial impression. Of course this must be seen in the context of the opening prayer: "your kingdom come". It is not any form of confidence that is appropriate, but confidence rooted in a bleief that God's new era is breaking out. Again, material prudence is attacked, anxiety is forbidden. Be like the ravens and the lilies, who don't have savings accounts and pension schemes, but just live, beautifully. Those who need to be told this are "of little faith": they imitate the pagans. Faith sounds like primitive "naturalness": disdain for bourgeois carefulness. But an intense spiritual prudence is required. One must be like the man who builds his house on rock not sand, and like the man who makes sure he can afford to build a tower before he gets going. This cause requires total commitment, self-discipline.

Matthew's Gospel is full of apocalyptic hints; there is much talk of good and evil being fully separated at a future time; for now we must live with their seeming inextricability. The message that all things are possible through faith is repeated in hyperbolic terms: if you really have faith you can tell a mountain to throw itself into the sea, and it will happen. Faith is again an attitude of incautious confidence. The parable of the talents is the most vivid example (Matthew 25): we are to trust that life is a fertile arena, a place where goodness naturally increases. We should express such confidence by risking everything. Such action is not seen as risky but as trusting. It is a grave sin to hinder this natural process of growth.

Does the faith that Jesus teaches involve having a view of Jesus as the Son of God, or the Messiah? In general, no, but when Peter identifies him as "the Christ, the Son of the living God", Jesus assents, but tells Peter not to broadcast this. The writer of the Gospel seems to be addressing the contradiction that although Jesus did not present himself in this way, it is how Christians are meant to see him. Although it was not part of the faith he openly taught, it is a key part of Christian faith.

John's Gospel stands apart from the other three: its idea of faith is influenced by Greek philosophy. The writer overlays the material we have already considered with the idea that faith resembles philosophical enlightenment. Those who recognize Jesus as "the Word" and "the light" are "children of God". In effect, faith is assent to the doctrine of the incarnation. In this Gospel it feels as if Jesus is *always* walking on water. He has a lofty manner, and enjoys theologizing. God has sent his son, says Jesus, "so that whoever believes in him shall not perish but have eternal life" (John 3:16). There is much polemic against the Jews' failure to recognize their Messiah. The earthy parables about seeds and servants are omitted, and so the idea of faith as an attitude of radical affirmation and trust in natural plenitude is eclipsed by this doctrine of the supernatural status of Christ. (This tends to be the favourite Gospel of churchmen, for this Jesus is practically posing for a stained-glass window.)

Can we summarize the teaching of Jesus in regard to faith? He radicalized the idea that God must be trusted absolutely: one must give and risk everything for the sake of serving him, through loving behaviour – respect for the old laws is secondary to this. And he tied this attitude to a revolutionary-apocalyptic worldview, in which God's victory over Satan is becoming manifest, in which the world is pregnant with God's kingdom, with the old prophetic vision of a new era of peace and justice. There are also hints that faith entails suffering, giving up security and even one's life, but much of this theme was surely added after Jesus's death, when the first Christians were steeling themselves against persecution. The meaning of Jesus is well summed up by the Roman Catholic theologian Herbert McCabe: his mission was "to be the future in the present" (McCabe 2002: 176).

Soon after Jesus's death, a movement emerged that preserved his teaching and added a new central feature: he had been raised up by God from the dead. This is how Paul puts it, in one of the earliest Christian texts (even earlier than the Gospels), his letter to Christians in Galatia. Here Paul explains the meaning of this event: it widens God's dealings with humanity, from the Jews to everyone. He says that, in a direct revelation, God told him to preach the Gospel to gentiles. He speaks of the "freedom we have in Christ Jesus" (Galatians 2:4), which includes the non-necessity of circumcision. For "a man is not justified by observing the law but by faith in Christ Jesus" (Galatians 2:16). He cites the passage from Genesis we noted earlier: Abraham "believed God and it was credited to him as righteousness". He backs this up with a quote from the prophet Habakuk: "The righteous will live by faith" (Galatians 3:11). The Jewish law has been elbowed aside, and the blessing given to Abraham has been made available to gentiles. All can now be "sons of God". What does this mean? Does believing in Christ make people morally perfect, in a way that the law never could? No, but it means that we are assuming the right attitude: "By faith we eagerly await through the Spirit the righteousness for which we hope" (Galatians 5:5). A new era is dawning, a "new creation": Christian faith is rooted in this "eschatological" awareness. It means trusting that God is initiating a cosmic revolution, and that we can be on the right side of it.

In a letter to the converts he has made in Corinth, Paul touches on an aspect of faith familiar to modern thought: it is in conflict with the dominant account of rationality. It sounds like foolishness, especially to the Greeks. But God is trumping worldly wisdom with this foolishness, just as he trumps worldly strength with his weakness. His power is hidden in the form of weakness, and his truth is hidden in the form of foolishness. This is perhaps the Bible's first acknowledgement that faith and reason might be in conflict. (There is a similar hint in the words of the man whose son Jesus heals in Mark: "Lord, I believe, help my unbelief" [Mark 9:24].) *Of course* it exceeds human rationality, this message that, through one crucified Jew, God is bringing a cosmic revolution, remaking humanity! The task of Christians is to preach this, primarily by the way they live. They must be squeaky clean, so that enemies of the new religion don't have ammunition for linking this new freedom with immorality. "Everything is permissible – but not everything is beneficial" (1 Corinthians 10:23): Paul is a sort of libertarian puritan. We shouldn't make rules about what is morally pure, but we should be incredibly careful not to seem morally slack.

But what is it that Christians are meant to have faith in? What is this cosmic happening that's dawning? One aspect of it is a new version of the Jewish belief in "the resurrection of the dead". Some in Corinth have doubted this, and Paul says it is crucial: it makes sense of Christ's resurrection. The risen Christ is the advance party of this general raising. "For as in Adam all die, so in Christ all will be made alive" (1 Corinthians 15:22). Christ will return to kick this event off. It will culminate in the destruction of death itself. We will all have new, spiritual bodies. His writing rises to a strange poetic intensity as he assures his hearers of this final mystery: there is some theatrical rhetoric in which he seems to reveal a vision he has had, in which the last trumpet sounds and we are "raised imperishable" (1 Corinthians 15:42), and he quotes Isaiah: "Death has been swallowed up in victory" (1 Corinthians 15:54). We are told that God will destroy all contrary and competing power, which could either mean that the ungodly are cancelled out, or that they are reclaimed as God's.

Well, how is anyone expected to believe all this? Does Paul expect his hearers to accept this exotic apocalyptic poem as the way it will be? It's worth noting that this vision of the end is consciously poetic. In effect Paul is saying: here is a way of imagining the final victory of God. We will all feature in a perfect new creation. It is also worth noting that this is not a belief in each soul's passage to an afterlife, to heaven or hell. There is not an "afterlife realm" coexisting with history: there is one big future event, of divine cosmic victory. The defeat of death is obviously crucial. He also quotes Hosea: "Where, O death, is your victory?/ Where, O death, is your sting?" (1 Corinthians 15:55). There is a ritualistic feel to this. What I mean is that the act of saying it has weight. It produces a moment of heightened confidence in the idea, as if its truth is already tasted *now*. In other words Paul is not just saying "here is the Christian doctrine of the end-time, you must believe in *x*, *y* and *z*". He is performing this faith for them in a little burst of virtuoso rhetoric. The idea of the end-time belongs to this mode of speaking. In other words, we have to resort to the poetic and ritual use of language, if we are to express this ultimate hope.

So Christian faith centres on this vague supernatural event, this sort of rhetorical icon, of God's final victory. We are meant to trust in this good cosmic outcome, which demands to be represented in violently mythical terms. It won't do to say, "I believe the natural goodness of humanity will prevail", or suchlike: we must assert this myth. On the other hand it is not sufficient just to assert this myth. For even more important than faith and hope is love. This business of faith only makes sense in the context of a new way of being: a readiness for the new order that is defined by putting love first. Let loving behaviour be the sign that your life is faith based, Paul is saying.

In a further letter to the Corinthians Paul says that God has "set his seal of ownership on us, and put his Spirit in our hearts as a deposit, guaranteeing what is to come" (2 Corinthians 1:22). This presents faith as a sort of miracle, of divine origin. How can we hold to this idea of God's salvation through Christ, in defiance of reason and tradition? No human effort could do it, so it must be God's doing. This is a clever way of building up a frail faith: reconceptualizing it as God's action in us. Soon he contrasts the day-to-day experience of suffering with the new, victorious identity that awaits the Christian. "So we fix our eyes not on what is seen, but on what is unseen. For what is seen is temporary, but what is unseen is eternal" (2 Corinthians 4:18); "We live by faith, not by sight" (2 Corinthians 5:7). Christians are those to whom God has promised something. Abrahamic impersonation is never far from Paul's mind. There is an element of dramatic role play. We ordinary people are, through faith, like biblical heroes. We have a secret, virtual identity. We are on a dramatic journey, away from old securities, towards the semi-unknown that God has promised us. He also likens the believer to an athlete, with his eyes on the prize, and to a soldier.

His letter to the Romans is largely a repetition of what he told the Galatians. The essence of Judaism was not outward observance but faith, and God has now universalized this. Even more keenly than before, Paul uses Abraham as a stick with which to beat "the law". This founding hero lived before the law was revealed. So he is our figurehead, our proof. Ironically this first Jew is the figurehead of *gentile* faith especially: "he is the father of all who believe but have not been circumcised" (Romans 4:11). Soon he builds to another poetic crescendo. In our mundane sufferings

> we are more than conquerors through him who loved us. For I am convinced that neither death nor life, neither angels nor demons, neither the present nor the future, nor any powers, neither height nor depth, nor anything else in all creation, will be able to separate us from the love of God that is in Christ Jesus our Lord. (Romans 8:37–9)

In a sense Paul's main purpose is to make little verbal icons of faith, often recycling phrases from the Old Testament. (It is no exaggeration to say that he is the most successful poet of all time, in that his little verbal icons are in daily use by millions.) Language is faith's medium. "Faith comes from hearing the message" (Romans 10:17), and it is expressed by re-proclaiming it, confessing it. In place of the law, Paul locates religion in this rhetorical process; the message is heard, believed, re-told. Faith is all about a reversal that God will effect. It is through language that we anticipate this reversal, that we make it already real, or virtually real.

The letter to the Hebrews contains the famous description of faith: "the assurance of things hoped for, the conviction of things not seen" (Hebrews 11:1). There follows a hymn to the Old Testament heroes of faith, who are still waiting, alongside us, for the final fulfilment of the promise.

Remember that passage from Sam Harris's book that we quoted in Chapter 1? Please turn back to it, on page 14, for we are now equipped to contest it. He says that this description of faith "seems to render faith entirely self-justifying": if I really believe Nicole Kidman loves me, although we have never met, it must be true. He goes on that faith is "belief in, and life orientation toward, certain historical and metaphysical propositions". This is a muddled attack. On one level an imagined love affair with a film star is a decent analogy for faith, for the suitor needs an attitude of bold trust. But then he elbows his own analogy aside, and his own awareness that faith is a form of trust, and voices the crude assumption that faith is the same as belief in "propositions", which suggests quasi-scientific claims about the universe. (He is thus overlooking the distinction between belief and faith that we saw Eagleton and Žižek highlighting.) He was right the first time: faith resembles the boldness of love, the mad trust that one's desire for this person might cease to be just a subjective passion and become embodied truth. And an honest reading of Paul's letters will show that "historical and metaphysical propositions" are almost beside the point; the key thing is this intensification of God-trust, to the point of expecting an imminent cosmic revolution that we struggle to conceptualize.

4. Faith and reason

For the atheists of Chapter 1, faith is the supreme tool by which religion fixes itself in human minds: although there is no evidence for the truth of this or that holy teaching, one is told to believe it by faith, which means taking it on trust from the authority that teaches it, and willing oneself to assent. Our account of biblical faith gives a rather different picture: faith is an attitude of radical trust in God, which entails quasi-utopian hope. But to trust that God has a good plan for humanity, one has to believe in God in the first place, the atheist will reply. Surely one has been told of his existence by some flawed authority, which discourages awkward questions. It is hard to know how to respond to this, for the Bible seems to have little conception of rational scepticism. God is assumed to be the most real person in the world. As we have seen, one part of the Old Testament broadly resembles philosophical discourse, but still God's reality is assumed, rather than seen as something in need of substantiation. In the New Testament, too, this is the case. Paul is not passionately arguing that God exists, but that the God who is assumed to exist is doing this new thing, in Jesus, and is to be understood in this revolutionary new way, not the old way. Someone who approaches the New Testament saying "but surely the really big question is whether God exists at all" is missing the point. To grasp anything of what it is about, you have to put that question aside, and imaginatively enter the world in which God's existence is assumed. Otherwise your impression of Jesus or Paul will never progress beyond "sufferer of the God delusion".

The Bible has no conception that belief in God is philosophically problematic (with the possible exception of Paul's awareness that the Gospel is folly to the Greeks). But, as we have seen, there is a recurrent idea that full-scale faith in God is defiant of common sense, convention; the hero of faith must defy the assumptions of those around him. He must risk himself, suffer isolation. He must take issue not with the scientific method but with a more general idea of reasonability.

This is relevant to the relationship between faith and reason in the Christian centuries, which we are surveying in this chapter. There is a necessary conflict between faith and reason, I shall argue, but to understand it we must keep "reason" open to its wider, everyday use. Rationality is tied up with the concepts of *common sense*, and *realism*, and therefore with an attitude of conventional caution. Remember the examples of faith we gave in the introduction: the idealistic teacher, and the couple moving house. Their faith does not come into conflict with rationality in the strict sense, but in the loose sense: conventional wisdom, worldly wise realism, the pragmatism of safety first.

As we shall see, Christian faith repeatedly seeks to renew itself by kicking against rationality (and reasonability and realism); by reasserting the primacy of faith. But, as we shall also see, what is really interesting about the tension between faith and reason in modern thought is that it spills out beyond "religion": it affects literature, philosophy and politics in very dramatic ways – from *Hamlet* to Hitler. The most important intellectual movement over the past century has been a reaction against the assumptions of the rationalist Enlightenment, an acknowledgement that faith must be reckoned with.

Is there a pagan version of faith?

While the Jews were putting faith at the heart of their identity, did this theme play any role in the religion and thought of the rest of the ancient world? Ancient Greek religion was based around local cults, and sacred sites devoted to a particular god. The core practice was sacrifice: giving the god something valuable in order to secure his or her favour. Such practices, which were built into the agricultural calendar, expressed gratitude and trust. The common practice of offering the first fruits to the gods sets up a gift-relation to nature; the giver feels assured of being given more the next year. Similarly, it was believed that the local deity protected the town, and that rituals had to be carefully performed to ensure the continuation of this protection. Stories were told, and enacted, highlighting this protective power.

Religion was about trust, then, but what about faith? Did human heroes display an exceptional trust in the gods that could be called faith? Of course they displayed great courage, but the specifically psychological courage of faith, which always overlaps with recklessness, is not much in evidence. Hercules, for example, needs valour and strength but not faith. Homer's heroes are canny, shrewd and wary of trusting potential enemies. The Trojans lost the war through being foolishly trusting of the big horse they were given. Heroes must trust the gods who protect them, but this is not emphasized particularly. It is also a virtue to trust fate, but there is little choice about such trust. The great virtues are simply martial courage and loyalty to one's kinsmen. If Achilles has faith, it's a stubborn faith in his own brilliance. Odysseus is a bit more complex: he has a sort of faith that he will get home, and this sense of destiny brings self-discipline. But it is his wife, Penelope, who is the real hero of faith. She refuses to bend to the common-sense view that she must forget her husband and remarry. Her faith is rooted in the sexual sense: fidelity. For a man to be exceptionally faithful in this way would put a question mark over his macho heroism. So faith was seen as a female virtue: men are admired for doing things, and being cunning, and women are admired for staying true to their men. But the loyalty of women was potentially excessive; it could lead to violent disorder. There are various tales of women reacting badly to abandonment. When Jason leaves Medea for someone else she takes revenge by killing her children; this is echoed in Dido's tragedy. Intense fidelity can lead to bunny-boiling madness.

Ancient Greek myths about gods and heroes provoked the first philosophers. Were they true? Were these gods real? Socrates started a sceptical trend, and was accused of corrupting Athenian youth. And yet he respected traditional cultic practices. Nor did he reject religious belief: he wanted to reconcile it with rationality (he resembled a demythologizing theologian). He was absolutely certain of his right to cast doubt on everything, even to the point of accepting martyrdom. According to Plato, he told the jury that convicted him that he did not fear death: "you too must look forward to death with confidence, and fix your minds on this one belief, which is certain: that nothing can harm a good man either in life or after death, and his fortunes are not a matter of indifference to the gods" (Plato 1984: 76). In *Phaedo*, Socrates explains that the philosopher must train himself to believe in the soul's immortality. He must develop a whole attitude of confidence: this is not "a blind and foolish confidence", as one of his interlocutors suggests, but rationally founded (*ibid*.: 152). It is through being confident about immortality that he actually achieves it (non-philosophers have to go through a sort of purgatory, he suggests). Socrates admits that his colourful account of the afterlife is somewhat speculative, but it is "both a reasonable contention and a belief worth risking; for the risk is a noble one. We should use such accounts to inspire ourselves with confidence" (*ibid*.: 178).

So Platonic philosophy entails trust in the authority of rationality, or rather spiritual rationality (for this is not scientific empiricism), and this trust must be consciously built up. It is a way of seeing the world. In *Phaedo* one of Socrates' friends points out that swans seem to sing in pain before death: maybe a sign that the soul is not immortal (swans were thought to have prophetic powers). No, says, Socrates, the swan song should be understood as ecstatic expectation of the immortality to come. It is fear of death that leads people to think otherwise (*ibid.*: 138). This is an indication that one's trusting worldview determines one's interpretation of evidence. In effect he is saying: see the world with confidence in eternal reason.

It is a form of faith, or trust, that strongly insists that it is well grounded in reason. (It resembles the Old Testament wisdom tradition, but is of course far keener to argue its case.) What chiefly distinguishes it from mainstream biblical faith is the lack of a social dimension. Salvation is the wise man's ability to rise above deceptive passions: there is no idea that salvation must be a corporate thing, a new social world. In the *Republic*, Plato imagines an ideal society, but it is really a more orderly version of the status quo; there is no hunger for a revolution that brings justice for all. Indeed, this is the last thing that Greek philosophy wants, for its practitioners rely on slaves. And the Bible suggests that faith, in the full sense, is partly born from the experience of slavery. So faith is a slave-based virtue: the ability to imagine a totally good human future, of universal justice, comes out of the *need* to imagine this. Greek conservatism continues with Aristotle. He emphasizes that the good life is political, which is to say that it must conform to the nature of Greek politics: military values, citizenship for elite males, slavery. As theologian and philosopher Herbert McCabe says, ancient Jewish faith "was a huge human liberation compared to which the Athenian democracy was a game for rich boys played while their armies of slaves kept the real world going" (2002: 58).

The instinctive conservatism of pagan philosophy continued into Roman times. Stoicism follows Plato in claiming to be rational, and in teaching a discipline of trust in rationality. It is a creed for the ruling-class citizen, who must master his passions, and uphold good order. For Seneca, Philosophy is a benign goddess, in whose guidance one should trust. The wise man seeks to reform himself, but learns to accept the way the world is. For the Stoic emperor Marcus Aurelius, "Everything which happens, is right" (Marcus Aurelius 1983: 27). So trust is central to this worldview: trust that the world is fundamentally good, despite the trials it brings. These Stoics would see it as desperate folly to imagine an imminent transformation of the world. Trust in goodness, which is the essence of religion, must be rational. The theologian John D. Caputo puts it well:

> The Stoics were advising us to refuse religion, to refuse to make ourselves vulnerable, to have a calm *apatheia* (no passion), whereas in the religious sense of life all that calm is disturbed by a divine passion ... a restless stirring with the passion for the impossible. (2001: 29)

The gospel of confidence

By this time, Christianity had entered the Roman world. In the late second century the philosopher Celsus wrote a rebuttal of the new-ish faith. What irritated him was that it wanted to resemble a philosophy school, but refused to play by the rules. It proudly retained its deeply primitive aspects, its use of exorcisms, and trance-inducing flute music, and a belief in the magical power of Jesus's name. (Earlier critics including Pliny had linked Christianity to Bacchae-type rites.) So Celsus complains that Christian "thought" is essentially uncivilized: "The Christian teachers ... do not want to give or to receive reasons for what they believe. Their favourite expressions are 'Do not ask questions, just believe!' and 'Your faith will save you!'" (1987: 54). When challenged on the absurdity of believing in the resurrection of the body, "they take cover by saying 'Nothing is impossible with God'" (*ibid*.: 86). "Plato can justify his teaching; Christians say 'First believe [in Jesus Christ]'" (*ibid*.: 93). In many respects, he says, "there is nothing unusual about what they believe, except that they believe it to the exclusion of more comprehensive truths about God" (*ibid*.). Another philosopher, Galen, made the same complaint in his book *On Hippocrates' Anatomy*, rooting it in the nature of the Bible: "it is Moses' method, in his books, to write without offering proofs, saying 'God commanded, God spoke'" (in Wilken 1984: 72). Such complaints, echoed by many other philosophers, are amazingly similar to the complaints of today's atheists. To base a philosophical viewpoint on faith is simply indefensible!

These critics had a point, for theologians did seem to want it both ways: they edged away from Paul's rebuke to Greek wisdom, and highlighted affinities between Christianity and philosophy, putting the "*logos*" theme of John's Gospel centre stage. But of course when it suited them they fell back on the certainty of faith. Clement of Alexandria suggested that faith and knowledge complemented each other. Irenaeus was more cautious: it is better "that one should have no knowledge whatever of any one reason why a single thing in creation has been made, but should believe in God, and continue in his love, than that, puffed up through knowledge of this kind, he should fall away from that love which is the life of man" (in Stevenson & Frend 1987: 113–14). If Christianity allows faith to be elbowed aside by reasoning, its essence is destroyed. The point was made more forcefully by the North African theologian Tertullian: "What indeed has Athens to do with Jerusalem? What has the Academy to do with the Church? ... Away with all attempts to produce a Stoic, Platonic, and dialectical Christianity! ... When we believe we desire no further belief" (in *ibid*.: 167). He also said "I believe because it is absurd" (in Chadwick 1967: 93). He was not an uncurious fundamentalist, as these quotes suggest, but a serious thinker who feared Christianity losing its distinctiveness, and its air of intrinsic authority. He was reacting to the para-Christian movement Gnosticism, and to a theologian called Marcion who proposed a nicer version of God, shorn of his violent side.

But more important than any theologian in protecting the counter-rational intensity of faith was the fact of martyrdom. When someone chose to die rather than recant, he became a vivid advertisement for the assurance of faith, the clearest proof that this religion has certainty at its heart; why else would people die for it? Martyrs captured the imagination as powerfully as suicide bombers do in today's Middle East. All martyrdom is apocalyptic: it doesn't just assert that divine justice will repair present woes, it yells it in blood.

As the Christian Church stabilized, and became a fairly coherent organization generally free from persecution, a new problem arose: how to preserve the pure intensity of faith. The problem was that eccentrics with heretical views often seemed more dynamic. Some of these claimed prophetic inspiration, and had to be denounced. A prophet called Montanus was accused of being an evil lunatic in the late second century, and a century later another such figure called Mani emerged; he claimed to bring a new, fuller revelation from God. What made these people so dangerous to Christian orthodoxy was that they highlighted the frailty of Christian authority: wasn't this religion based on one man's claim to bring the definitive revelation? Why should one have faith in what the Church taught rather than what these new prophets taught? Theologians put new emphasis on the need to have faith in the Church, to trust in its time-tested reliability. The big theological development of the first few centuries of Christianity is that faith in the Church, its hierarchy and its teaching, becomes the central tenet of Christian faith. The essence of Catholicism is the belief that Christian faith is only fully authentic when it accepts the authority of the institution. In the early fourth century the Church became the dominant religion of the Roman Empire. If there is an institutional orthodoxy, backed by the state, can one still have a dynamic faith in the free God of

Paul? If this religion is part of the status quo, can it still be driven by expectation of the kingdom of God? Some thinkers responded to this question by heading for the desert and launching a new form of Christian radicalism: the ascetic movement.

In North Africa, the young Augustine was also responding to this question, in his way. Christianity was becoming the dominant ideology, and was therefore somewhat ordinary. His mother was a Christian, which put him off for years. He flirted with Gnosticism and pagan philosophy, and sneered at Christianity on aesthetic grounds: it seemed too crude. For a while he opted for the more exotic, and less morally rigorous, Manichean faith. In his *Confessions* he looks back on his spiritual adolescence, which he often calls his "wandering", which also means "erring". He carefully analyses his restless angst, his long refusal to "come home" to the true faith. He is rootless and restless until he finally hears God speaking to him through Scripture, and accepts the authority of the Church. Although this is a narrative of someone being called by God it is really the opposite of a biblical call narrative, for all the interest comes before the call. Augustine is the opposite of Abraham, who is called to leave home and wander into adventurous new territory. Augustine wanders around, having adventures, *until* he is called to the stability of his mother's tradition. So Augustine's *Confessions* is addressing the problem that faith has become institutionalized; it is not a place for Abrahams or Josephs, for receivers of fresh revelation. But there is still dynamism, and unprecedented self-discovery, in the act of discovering one's need for this stability.

So what pulls him "home"? He becomes sick of the corrosive doubt that all other philosophical positions seem to accept as inevitable. For years, this doubt seemed part of manly realism, and there seemed something feminine about yielding to divine authority. He became a city slicker, a lawyer and spin-doctor, a spiritual *flâneur*, proud of his freedom. But his explorations in philosophy produced angst. Ethical relativism bothered him: the impossibility of finding an objective morality. Looking back, he explains that Christianity overcomes this, not by delivering permanent answers, but by focusing our attention on what is beyond all human moral conventions: "Can it at any time or place be unjust 'to love God'?" (Augustine 1991: 54). Morality is generally ruled by human convention, "but when God commands a thing to be done, against the customs or compact of any people, though it were never done by them before, it is to be done" (*ibid.*: 55). What chiefly converts him is a growing admiration for the *style* of Christian thought: it boldly refers to God's authority. For years he had an aversion to this, akin to the modern liberal's. But he realizes that other positions claim a sort of authority for themselves too, without quite admitting it. This is especially true of Manicheanism, a blend of mystical religion and philosophical theory, which he finally rejects as dishonest.

> I thought it more modest and not in the least misleading to be told by the Church to believe what could not be demonstrated … rather than from the Manichees to have a rash promise of knowledge with mockery of mere belief, and then afterward to be ordered to believe many fabulous and absurd myths impossible to prove true.   (*Ibid.*: 95)

Christianity is upfront about the role that authority plays in it, whereas other positions entail faith in a vaguer sense (Marxism would be a good example of a modern position that is rooted in an awkward half faith that it does not honestly admit to). His full conversion is a matter of hearing authority in God's (scripturally mediated) voice, and trusting that the Church is the guardian of this voice. This theme continues in *The City of God*. Pagan religion and philosophy is weak, muddled: Christianity is confident, forceful.

Augustine's conversion can be seen in psychosexual terms. He begins by assuming that faith is for weak women; it is a fantasy of patriarchal authority that appeals to them. To accept it threatens one's masculinity. But he comes to feel that he needs this authority. To some extent this entails abandoning macho independence and accepting vulnerability, but one also finds a new male strength by participating in this rhetoric of authority, rather than being passive to it.

Augustine's theology continued the tradition of having it both ways, in respect of philosophy. Christianity was the fulfilment of Greek philosophy, yet faith in revelation was necessary. In the following centuries, as the Church gained power, the claim that this religion was rationally founded became ever stronger, for philosophy was effectively owned by theology. It was impossible to question the idea that reasoning supported faith. Faith was still necessary, but there was little sense that it was a counter-rational leap; there was no non-religious reason to kick against. In consequence, there was no place for the Pauline idea that faith is folly in the eyes of philosophy.

But this did not mean that faith was colonized by reason (it was the other way round). The Church was careful to defend Christian doctrine from a rationalist drift. Many of the heresies it batted off were attempts to reduce the scandalously counter-rational nature of this religion. The doctrine of the Trinity was asserted at the First Council of Nicaea against a movement, Arianism, that wanted to lessen Christ's status. And one of the heresies that Augustine fought, Pelagianism, suggested that sin has no necessary power over us, that we can progress to moral perfection. By insisting that we are always sinners, reliant on God's grace, Augustine was putting faith before either right conduct or reason.

Towards modernity

In the Middle Ages learning waned, and the Church increased its power over what remained. When philosophy revived somewhat, in the twelfth century, it was in the form of a system of Christian rationalism called scholasticism, which made great use of Aristotle's thought (reintroduced to Europe by Muslim scholarship). In the following century Thomas Aquinas developed a grand system that claimed to prove God's existence in terms of the Aristotelian concept of "being". He did not claim that the specifics of Christian doctrine could be proved, so faith was still required. But he showed that philosophy vouched for a good and all-powerful creator God.

This provoked a reaction known as nominalism. According to the Oxford theologian William of Ockham, it was folly to create a grand rational system within which God operated. We don't know anything of God through reason, but are totally reliant on faith. He was attacking more than just Aquinas's work, or scholasticism. As we have seen, theology had tended in this rationalist direction ever since the second century; it had repressed the idea that God might be at odds with rationality. A brief look at the Bible suggests that the Judaeo-Christian God is obviously at odds with rational philosophy, but this could not be admitted, emperor's-new-clothes style. The nominalists dared to point it out. For Ockham, the world is not an orderly intelligible system; it exists just because God wills it to exist. His central concept was the freedom of God's will. There was a sudden new emphasis on the individual's need for faith. Christianity was not a religion of trust in divine reason, he said, but of faith in the biblical God. One needed to confront the *improbability* of his saving plan for humanity. The Church tried to suppress this unsettling movement, which seemed so close to scepticism.

At the same time (the fourteenth century), mystical writing became popular: this was another way of recovering the drama of individual faith, and it implied a critique of Christianity as an ecclesiastical and philosophical system. For mystics, faith is a personal, emotional thing, and it involves the whole body. Mystics experience physical echoes of the sufferings of Jesus, and yearn for union with God in a quasi-sexual way. Women writers were particularly prominent, including Julian of Norwich, whose lovely distillation of biblical prophecy – "all will be well ..." – we have already noted. She receives communications from God, like a biblical prophet, but they feel rather homely and unthreatening. Perhaps mysticism was largely female because male prophetic speech was likely to be seen as too threatening to the Church. But some appeared none-theless, under the thin cover of "literature"; in William Langland's *Piers Plowman*, myticism blended with a tradition of anticlerical political protest.

This upsurge of popular devotion was an important part of the Renaissance, especially in northern Europe. But it was balanced by the better-known face of the Renaissance, neoclassical humanism. The Italian intellectuals emphasized reason, moderation and civic order, like the Stoics they dusted down.

Desideratus Erasmus, the intellectual giant of the early fifteenth century, tried to combine both strains. Personal faith was crucial, he taught, and this was the real goal of learning: that people of all classes should deepen their faith. He urged the Church to reform its dry, official, over-rational theology, in order to keep popular piety onside. Also, it must incorporate the new insights yielded by careful reading of the New Testament.

Martin Luther agreed, but it gradually dawned on him that the rediscovery of authentic Christian faith could not be accommo-dated by the old structures. He was an academic monk, schooled in nominalist philosophy and scriptural study. For years he strug-gled with a distinctly nominalist dark night of the soul: God seemed unknowable, unpleasant and unpleasable – terrifying. The rigour of monastic life was really just a shot in the dark, a mere guess at how God might want to be served. His turning point came through reading the passages of Paul's letters that we discussed earlier, espe-cially Paul's citation of Habakuk: "the righteous man shall live by faith". The key to salvation is simply trusting that God is good, that all will be well, that he will save us. That's all. No more. That's all he asks of us. What a relief! All the rigmarole of religious life is irrelevant; worse, it obscures this, the simple key to our salvation. And so the young monk tried to point out that a revolution was necessary, for the very essence of Christianity had been pushed to the margins by Church orthodoxy, which implied that righteousness comes by obeying its rules, swallowing its doctrines, revering its officials. If we take Paul seriously, the whole system is blown away. At first Luther tried to reform from within. He pointed out that the Church's system of indulgences (buying forgiveness from the pope) was a denial of the biblical idea that each believer relied solely on God's grace: shouldn't this issue be … looked into? His stand only got him into trouble, so he lost faith in the institution.

He set about reinventing Christianity around the concept of faith. The purpose of the Church is to spread the message that salvation comes through faith. He urged Germany's leaders to throw out the Roman Church and set up a new Church that told the truth. He revived Paul's disdain for the law, for holy rules. Salvation cannot be earned through any form of action. All the emphasis must be on faith, on accepting that God does it all, that he freely chooses to save us.

Luther realized that he had an iconic role: he became famous when he refused to recant in front of the emperor, like an Old Testament prophet. He showed that he scorned pragmatism and safety and trusted God. Of course, he had no blueprint for remaking the Church, and this was a plus-point: it showed that God was in control. Luther's revolt was consciously based in a dramatic, reckless performance of faith.

For Luther, faith is simply a matter of hearing, and wanting to pass on, God's message to us, his promise of salvation. As for Paul, faith is a positive response to this communication, which entails the desire to communicate it. The idea that he calls for faith in the Bible misses the point: you have to have faith in the message, the promise, which is rooted in the Bible as a whole, and is explicitly expressed in certain bits of it (primarily Paul). But the point is not to gaze up at scriptural authority, on its pedestal, but to take it down, open it up, make it live, treat it like a play script, to be re-performed.

Anyone who has read as much as a page of Luther will know that he is the most fiery of polemicists. In his polemical exchange with Erasmus he reflects on the need for a Christian to have an assertive style, rather than one of academic carefulness. Indeed the very essence of faith is a willingness to assert, he says.

> Take the Apostle Paul – how often does he call for that "full assurance" which is, simply ... the highest degree of certainty and conviction? ... And what need is there of a multitude of proofs? Nothing is more familiar or more characteristic among Christians than assertion. Take away assertions, and you take away Christianity. Why, the Holy Spirit is given to Christians from heaven in order that He may glorify Christ ... The Spirit asserts to such purpose that He breaks in upon the whole world and convinces it of sin, as if challenging it to battle. (Luther 1957: 67)

What could be more offensive to liberal ears than this claim to speak aggressively on God's behalf? What saves Luther from being a mere theological thug is the fact that he actually has a complex understanding of the otherness of God's verbal authority. The Spirit might momentarily speak through us, but we never own it, for we never stop being error-prone human beings. Throughout his writing he represents the struggle of faith to stand up to the devil and other negative powers. It must respond by channelling God's authority, but this tough talk is an act, an effort. In one book he addresses Satan: "Sir Devil, I fear not thy threatenings and terrors, for there is one whose name is Jesus Christ, in whom I believe; he hath abolished the law, condemned sin, vanquished death, and destroyed hell ... This faith the devil cannot overcome, but is overcome of it" (1956: 28). A few lines later it is death he rebukes: "Thus when I feel the terror of death I say: Thou hast nothing to do with me, O death; for I have another death which killeth thee my death" (*ibid.*). The demonic forces are trying to undermine trust in God's promises; one can only see them off by referring to God's power: "Whoever, without the word of grace and prayer, disputes with the devil touching sin and law, will lose. [For he is] a crafty rhetorician" (1995: 299). Faith is an ongoing rhetorical struggle, in which the believer echoes, or participates in, the power of God. He is not in possession of this power, but dependent on it. This entails self-criticism, for one is always rebuking aspects of oneself: one's gloom, or doubt, or selfishness, "for each one of us is himself a great and spacious sea, filled with reptiles and animals" (Luther 1959: 37). Gloom was a particular bugbear for Luther: the devil's most predictable guise. Faith means dispelling it, not only by quoting scripture but also by having fun with one's wife and children, and enjoying music: defiantly enjoying God-given pleasures. Dreary modern psychology would label him manic-depressive, or bipolar, or something: maybe he is just more alertly human than most of us, ever-conscious of selfhood as a dramatic struggle.

This "dialogic" dynamic (meaning that voices are sparring) makes faith surprisingly open. It is legitimate, indeed pious, to voice one's objections and doubts, and one's ungodly thoughts and moods, as part of acknowledging one's need for God. There is no escaping the endless tension between faith's acceptance of the word of God and the quibbles of "the flesh" (meaning all of one's fallen humanity). Faith necessitates this inner dialogue.

And this dynamic is not as counter-rational as it superficially seems. Although Luther sometimes rebukes "reason", or "Mistress Reason", as if it's a demonic force, he really means "that form of reason that sneers at the idea of God's grace". In fact this dialogue structure is a way of airing rational objections rather than suppressing them.

So faith, for Luther, is a psychological style. It is an attitude of confidence – defiant, embattled confidence – that God's cause will triumph, that one can be part of this. And it is intrinsically agonistic: it is a perpetual struggle against the voices that mock this narrative – and these negative voices inhabit one's psyche. This clash of inner voices is known as psychomachy. One of Luther's central achievements was to put this dynamic at the very heart of faith. I consider his dramatic, positive voice the greatest product of Christendom, worth a hundred cathedrals.

This inner drama became an important feature of Protestantism over the next century, and it also found secular expression in the birth of modern drama; allow me a tiny excursion on Shakespeare. In various plays, but above all *Hamlet*, Shakespeare foresees a clash between faith and reason. His most famous tragic hero is an uncanny prediction of the fate of faith in modernity: it will be marginalized, made powerfully problematic, impossible to accommodate, yet will also be the source of the highest fascination. The sullen prince experiences, up on the battlements, a secular version of the prophetic call, and commits himself totally to his dark, secret mission, which is to purify culture as well as to kill his uncle. He promises to remember the ghost's words:

> Yea, from the table of my memory
> I'll wipe away all trivial fond records,
> All saws of books, all forms, all pressures past
> That youth and observation copied there,
> And thy commandment all alone shall live
> Within the book and volume of my brain,
> Unmix'd with baser matter ...   (*Hamlet* I.v)

His new duty entails the suppression of rationality (there's also an echo of Paul putting away childish things). He must will himself to obey this quasi-divine calling. He then meets his friend Horatio, and in flighty excitement tells him, "There are more things in heaven and earth, Horatio, / Than are dreamt of in your philosophy" (I.v). The play shows him struggling to cope with his secret, his "faith": the humanist in Hamlet wishes he were free of it. But the play does not side with rational enlightenment against the dark superstition of faith for the ghost is real, and Hamlet is a hero in his honest acceptance of his inner struggle. The pedestal on which this play has (rightly!) been put over the centuries is a sign that our tradition continues to see the highest value in the drama of faith. (Those who talk about Shakespeare's possible Catholicism should note his fascination with the most Protestant of themes.)

Lutheran psychomachy also found more directly Christian literary expression in the poetry of George Herbert and John Donne, and in the prose of John Bunyan. But by Bunyan's time, the mid-seventeenth century, a new age of philosophical enquiry was underway, and the vigorous style of faith was in danger of looking rather primitive. A new type of thinker was prioritizing rationality in a way that threatened the whole idea of Christian revelation. Philosopher and mathematician René Descartes offered a new basis for rationality, in the individual mind. Political philosopher Thomas Hobbes offered a rational view of human history and politics; lens-grinder and philosopher Baruch Spinoza offered a sort of spiritualized rationalism. Such thought led to a new assumption: that religion must base itself on reason. Polymath Thomas Browne warned, "They who would prove Religion by Reason, do but weaken the cause which they endeavour to support", but the spirit of the age ignored this. Almost no one actually professed atheism, but these new philosophies reduced God to a mere rational principle. The new rational theology was known as deism. It wanted to play down, or even reject, the supernatural elements in Christianity, and assert its compatibility with the rationality of nature, whose laws were being discovered by Isaac Newton and others. This approach flourished within the Church of England, partly because the English were tired of religious extremism after their civil war.

Deism also crept into French religious culture, despite the dominance of the Catholic Church. Blaise Pascal was a scientific genius who developed an eccentric religious streak. He joined a movement called Jansenism, which emphasized personal faith and opposed Jesuit authoritarianism (although it was Catholic it resembled a form of Protestantism). Soon after he died in 1662 his religious reflections, the *Pensées*, were published. The book is a brilliant attack on the deist reconciliation of Christianity and rationality. No one had ever thought so clearly and so carefully about the tension between faith and reason, and about the danger of collapsing this tension in a convenient but intellectually dishonest synthesis.

He begins by insisting that reason is fallible, patchy, and that morality is subject to convention, and even fashion (Augustine had the latter insight, as we saw). So it is wrong to think that reason can be the basis for religion. "There is no certainty, apart from faith, as to whether man was created by a good God, an evil demon, or just by chance" (Pascal 1976: §131). Atheism and deism are "almost equally abhorrent to Christianity" (*ibid.*: §449), for deism implies that faith is unnecessary, a mere add-on. "It is the heart which perceives God and not the reason. That is what faith is: God perceived by the heart, not by the reason" (*ibid.*: §424). The unique thing about Christianity is that it insists on this distinction: "Faith is a gift from God. Do not imagine that we describe it as a gift of reason. Other religions do not say that about their faith. They offered nothing but reason as a way to faith, and yet it does not lead there" (*ibid.*: §588). This echoes Augustine's rejection of pseudo-rational Manicheanism. "Philosophers and all the religions and sects in the world have taken natural reason for their guide. Christians alone have been obliged to take their rules from outside themselves" (*ibid.*: §769).

Does this mean that reason has no positive role at all in religion? No, for of course Pascal is *reasoning* about the nature of faith. And sometimes he highlights this: "Submission and use of reason. That is what makes true Christianity" (*ibid*.: §167); "It is your own inner assent and the consistent use of your reason rather than that of others which should make you believe" (*ibid*.: §505). The believer has to develop a new sort of reasoning, moulded to his faith. The problem with general reasoning is that it assumes it has the right to explain everything; it wants to be the master-discourse. At one point he echoes the "dialogic" structure of Luther's faith:

> [One] carries on an interior dialogue with oneself, which it is important to keep under proper control ... We must keep silence as far as we can and only talk to ourselves about God, whom we know to be true, and thus convince ourselves that he is. (*Ibid*.: §536)

His faith stemmed from a conversion experience in 1654, a mystical vision. He wrote a short report of this, presumably just after it occurred: a sort of prose-poem of praise, which he seems to have carried with him ever-afterwards, sewn into his clothes. It includes the line: "'God of Abraham, God of Isaac, God of Jacob', not of philosophers and scholars" (*ibid*.: §913).

Despite his suspicion of enlightened rationalism, Pascal was no reactionary who thought that modern science could simply be condemned: instead he insisted on a sort of barrier protecting the discourse of faith from that of reason. He saw the necessity for separate development: apartheid. Christianity must stop claiming to be essentially rational, for the weakness of this claim leaves it terribly vulnerable. Furthermore, the claim obscures the essence of Christianity, which is faith.

But he was going against the grain. In early-eighteenth-century England, deism was so strong that even the Archbishop of Canterbury agreed that Christianity's irrational elements were dangerous irrelevances. True faith was a matter of rational self-interest, not the "enthusiasm" of the fanatic. The deists used "enthusiasm" as we use "extremism". This trend influenced French Enlightenment essayist Voltaire, who visited England in 1726. Back in France, he attacked the thought of Pascal, calling it a dark, misanthropic throwback to medieval pessimism. What sort of God demanded that we abandon reason for blind faith? Instead we must trust our rationality, trust that it is a divine gift, and that it can make the world a better place. A new rational–moral religion was needed; progress depended on a religious reverence for reason. Trust was needed, but not faith.

> What is faith? Is it to believe what appears evident? No. It is evident to me that there is a necessary, eternal, supreme, intelligent being. This is not a matter of faith, but of reason ... Faith consists in believing, not what appears to be true, but what appears to our understanding to be false.
>
> (Voltaire 1971: 208)

This ideology of divine rationality was just what eighteenth-century society wanted, especially in England: it allowed the old religious forms to coexist with the new secularism (and its new capitalism, as we saw). It provided an umbrella under which believers and sceptics could all get along. But soon a new sort of philosopher dissented: David Hume smelled a lazy fudge. The whole idea of divine reason is a myth; the honest philosopher can see that rationality is a shaky, incomplete thing that can be subtly twisted by human agendas. And the idea that it supports traditional religion is absurd. Although an atheist, he was in a sense reviving the nominalist attack on the scholastic system, which claimed to reconcile reason and divine truth. Let us be honest: religious belief is at odds with rationality. In his essay *Of Miracles* he makes this plain:

> The Christian religion not only was at first attended with miracles, but even at this day cannot be believed by any reasonable

person without one. Mere reason is insufficient to convince us of its veracity. And whoever is moved by *Faith* to assent to it, is conscious of a continued miracle in his own person, which subverts all the principles of his understanding, and gives him a determination to believe what is most contrary to custom and experience. (1963: 226)

This could have been written by Pascal in defence of faith, and the sentiment echoes Luther. One of the very few theologians to see the positive side of Hume was the eccentric German theologian J. G. Hamann, who wrote: "Hume may have said this with a scornful and critical air, yet this is orthodoxy and witness to the truth from the mouth of an enemy" (in Liebrecht 1966: 43). Hamann was an influence on Kierkegaard, who, as we shall see, revived this frail anti-deism tradition.

But the intellectual tide was still with deism: science seemed to confirm the benign creator, the natural law-maker. The argument from design – the argument that the world must have been created by a divine intelligence – was a central pillar of the ideology of the age. As you may have heard, it was eventually undermined by Charles Darwin. The year of writing, 2009, is the bicentenary of his birth, and atheist intellectuals have been queuing round the block to explain his revolution to us. Unfortunately they tend to be unaware of the tension within theology that we have been discussing; they assume that theology was, and is, synonymous with natural theology: with the claim that God is provable. These atheists do not understand the complex tradition rooted in nominalism, Luther, Pascal and others, which has *already* attacked deism from the theological side, and is therefore *not* undermined by Darwin.

German theology made a half-turn away from deism. Kant taught that natural science was unable to establish God's reality, but that moral philosophy *was* able to do so. Like Voltaire, he held that a rational religion could unite humanity. God should be understood as the universal moral imperative. This entails purging him of his irrational side. Thus Caputo: "God is brought before the court [of Reason], like a defendant with his hat in his hand, and required to give an account of himself, to show his ontological papers, if he expects to win the court's approval" (2001: 46). To be a credible modern universal religion, Christianity must drop its embarrassing old claim to be revealed.

The German idealist G. W. F. Hegel developed this approach, with more nuance. A reinvented Christianity must understand that truth is social and historical; the fact of radical cultural development must be factored in. The point is that God is expressed through the story of progress towards the true social and rational religion. And such progress is not smooth but involves contradiction. This tradition moves forwards by turning itself inside out. So Christianity, which is rational and social, necessarily has an irrational and individualistic side, which it kicks against. The lonely, irrational faith of Abraham and others is not a model for us now: it was a necessary stage of alienation, which he calls "the unhappy consciousness", which the Jews are still suffering from. True religion overcomes this, and is socially well adjusted.

This future-oriented philosophy, about a contradiction moving towards a resolution, sparked Marx. His thought launched a new and destructive chapter in the history of faith, in which faith became disguised as a new form of saving science. In the 1940s German-Jewish philosopher Karl Löwith analysed this very acutely.

The Communist Manifesto is, first of all, a prophetic document, a judgement, and a call to action and not at all a purely scientific statement based upon the empirical evidence of tangible facts … It is the old Jewish messianism and prophetism … which explain the idealistic basis of Marx's materialism … The *Communist Manifesto* still retains the basic features of a messianic faith: "the assurance of things hoped for" … The

Communist creed, though a pseudo-morphosis of Judeo-Christian messianism, lacks the fundamentals of it: the free acceptance of humiliation and of redemptive suffering as the condition of triumph … The proletarian Communist wants the crown without the cross. (1949: 43–4)

Marx repressed his awareness of his religious debt, wanting to be a fully rational analyst of the world's future. He poured scorn on the utopian dreamers, insisting that only hard science mattered. We shall return to Marxist "faith" in the next chapter.

Hegelianism also provoked Kierkegaard, in the completely opposite way: he pronounced a nominalist–Pascalian "No!" Christianity is not a super-subtle version of rational moral progress – it actually stands in contrast to such arrogant thought. Hegel's system claimed to have understood the role of faith in the development of the true rational–social religion, but faith is not something to be understood; it is a passion to be suffered. We shall look at this "existentialist" approach in the next chapter.

Spilt faith

The dominance of rationalist philosophy and theology did not kill faith off: it led it to find new homes. As we have just seen, one of these was Marxism, although in this house it wasn't allowed to speak its name. It also migrated to the tradition we call "literature". As the Enlightenment progressed, and faith was being squeezed out of theology, literature acquired a huge new sense of its importance. To a large extent, it became the new home of faith. We have already seen this in relation to Wordsworth; it is just as evident in the other Romantics. William Blake, with his anticlerical and revolutionary sympathies, was reviving the radical dissenting Protestant tradition of the seventeenth century in the literary sphere. And

93

so, more tentatively, was Samuel Taylor Coleridge, who was a Unitarian preacher in his youth. Why didn't they pursue theology rather than literature? Partly because the discipline of theology had been too fully co-opted by deism. So they added to a new sense that literature was an alternative site of the individual's apprehension of the sacred. For some writers, this alternative site was anti-Christian: Shelley's poetry intensified the atheist–utopian side of deism. But he too was keen on the idea of the individual faith-hero, the prophet, the inspired bard, bringing new revelation. This could be called the essence of poetic Romanticism: the idea that this role had to be reinvented to save modern society from becoming a huge soulless machine.

Thomas Carlyle is a good example of Romanticism as a climate of thought based in the secularization of Protestant faith. He rejected the strict Calvinism in which he was raised, but remained shaped by it. He saw the essential engine of history as the heroic faith of the visionary leader. It doesn't matter what these visionaries have faith *in*, as long as they have it in spades, and so remake the world around them. He idolized all visionary strongmen, from Mohammed to the French revolutionaries. He was particularly keen on Protestants, chiefly Luther: the Reformation depended "only on the passionate voice of one man" (Carlyle 1966: 135). But his concern was to agree not with Luther's ideas, but with his heroic style, which was continued by Oliver Cromwell and others, and lives on in "German literature and the French revolution" (*ibid.*: 137). His strange new move was to empty faith of its content, and admire its form – and also to highlight its political efficacy. New movements needed leaders with a strong enough vision to inspire followers.

Soon something similar happened in philosophy, and it revolutionized the discipline. Friedrich Nietzsche went further than Carlyle; instead of just admiring the creative power of the individual visionary, he claimed to be a prophet, and not just any prophet but *the* prophet of modern times. Unlike Romantic poets, who hinted that they had some sort of prophetic role, but were vague about how this worked, he claimed to have a clear theory explaining it.

He was a strange sort of atheist. Unless you reject God *in the right way*, he said, you are still deluded. For Dawkins *et al.* this is nonsense: God doesn't exist, therefore atheists are simply factually right. Nietzsche didn't believe in such atheism. Why not? Because it failed to see that religion, in a wide sense, is true. In what "wide sense"? In the sense that we need meaning, we need myths, we need a sense of drama and ritual in our lives, whether it's chanting on a football terrace, raving on Ecstasy or cheering the Queen. Atheists who say religion is irrational are as subhuman as Dr Spock on *Star Trek*. They haven't noticed what life is like. Without knowing it, they subscribe to a new religion about progress towards a perfect rational–moral world, but this is full of all sorts of inane prejudices they have no inkling of. And it is indebted to Christian morality in ways they don't understand.

So how *should* we reject God? With awareness of the magnitude of what we are doing. Imagine a tense father–son relationship. The son grows up and has to reject the father's stifling claim to authority. If the son says, let's be reasonable, let's accept that we are two adults now, with an equal claim to authority, and therefore your claim to superior authority is inappropriate, he is missing the point. He has to supplant the father, usurp his claim to authority, fight him for it, wrest it from him. This is how Nietzsche sees his relationship with Christianity (his father was a Protestant minister). Unless atheism takes over the intensity and the authority that resides in Christianity, then it is a lesser thing than what precedes it. (In a sense the atheists of Chapter 1 have an inkling of this: they try to seem rude, bullish, swashbuckling, stylish in their rejection of God – this is a weak echo of Nietzsche. Even Dawkins may have some awareness of this: that to be widely heard he must play a sort of iconic, theatrical role.)

Nietzsche's new philosophy was all about the godlike confidence of the truly enlightened atheist. In a sense it all amounts to nothing more than: "Look at this voice; look how free and stylish it is!" Nietzsche's idea of freedom and style is heavily based on the voice of Protestant faith; he wants to outdo the prophetic voice that mediates divine authority. And one key aspect of this is a new attitude to rationality. To outdo God's voice, you have to outdo his cavalier approach to rationality. For otherwise one is confined to a deeply limited style. It's not enough to say "that old claim to authority contravenes reason"; one has to say "here is a better claim to authority".

So despite rejecting Christianity as a religion for weaklings, he actually admires aspects of it very much, in particular the Christian tradition that rejects the need for rational proofs, that is happy simply to assert God's authority. At one point he admits to admiring Jesus on these grounds: to him "dialectic [i.e. Socratic rationalism] is ... quite absent, as likewise the idea that any faith, any 'truth' can be proved by argument" (1968: 170). And he acknowledged that Luther's Protestantism contained an admirable rhetorical force, which the new atheism must learn from. But this strength is concealed beneath the massive error of humanity's inferiority to God. So essentially he wants to combine the Prometheanism of the Enlightenment with the prophetic and fideistic rhetoric of Protestantism. Humanity must liberate itself from the demeaning illusion of Christianity, *but can only do so by commandeering its prophetic tradition.*

On one level, Nietzsche's idea that he was a post-Christian prophet was just nuts (which is why he went nuts). But it is also true that he, more than anyone else, launched twentieth-century philosophy and the whole revolution known as postmodernism. The essence of this revolution is a rejection of the Enlightenment's confidence in reason. Every claim to talk about the human world with rational neutrality is lacking in self-knowledge. It fails to see that it is speaking for a certain power interest. It is like a little rich kid who says, and believes, that the economic system is rational. In a sense Marx got there first when he said that liberal ideology is a cover for capitalist power interest. But he failed to see that his claim to "science" was just as shaky. The same is true of Freud: he exposed deeper motivations, but calling psychoanalysis science is a blatant contravention of the Trade Descriptions Act. Nietzsche, on the other hand, exposed the self-deluding nature of conventional rationality, and of all possible rationality. Every "rational" explanation of the human is an exercise in deception.

So has every claim to rationality become illegitimate after Nietzsche? According to Caputo, a proper reading of his work should lead to "not the jettisoning of reason but a redemption of reason, one that is a lot more reasonable than the bill of goods about an overarching, transhistorical Rationality that the Enlightenment tried to sell us. For that is a highly unreasonable Reason" (2001: 63). So we can now have a more nuanced and humble idea of reason, wary of its own capacity for hubris.

Does this change the rules of faith's encounter with reason? It's hard to say. What is clear is that, in the twentieth century, the boundary between faith and reason becomes blurred in new ways. On one level this is progress away from rigid Enlightenment habits, but it has a dark side. For faith migrated into politics in a new way, with hellish results. The emergence of fascism was aided by the climate of thought that includes Carlyle and Nietzsche (and the modernist poetry of W. B. Yeats and Ezra Pound). And political adaptations of Darwin played a big role: strong men will "inevitably" arise to inspire strong nations. This is a pseudo-science with a role for faith, in the sense of will, belief.

This trend found its purest form in a book written in 1924. Hitler's *My Struggle* is a reaction to the erosion of faith in the modern world, owing to democracy, socialism and mechanistic capitalism. The latter are not opposites, but two sides of the same Jew-minted coin. It is time to rediscover the authentic traditional faith of nationhood, which is clearly a post-Protestant faith. Soulless modernity can only be routed by true nationalism, rooted in the individual's "inner pride" in his membership of it (Hitler 1937: 22). The key to revolution is the fact that "the people love a ruler more than a suppliant and feel more inwardly satisfied by doctrines which suffer no rival, than by an admission of liberal freedom" (*ibid.*: 23). Heroic individualism must assert itself against "the majority". The legacy of Protestantism is ambiguous: it "will always help in furthering all that is essentially German whenever it is a matter of inward purity or increasing national sentiment", but it fails to see that Judaism is the enemy (*ibid.*: 56). The essence of Hitlerism is nationalism as a personal passion, a faith. What principally stands in the way of this is the idea of universal human values, an international cause that claims to be morally superior to nationalism – and Marxism is the supreme expression of this. For most of this book, Hitler recounts his existential struggle to commit himself to revolutionary nationalism. He offers his faith as the pioneering model. The personal becomes political as never before: this is a political ideology based in his self-discovery.

He regrets the fact that people have drifted away from church allegiance, for people need religion. "If religious doctrine and faith really get a grip on the mass of the people, the absolute authority of that faith is then the whole basis of its efficacy" (*ibid.*: 114). He wants to create a nationalism that has learned from this; that feels like church. He was clearly influenced by the organic Catholic culture of Austria, with its assertive pomp. Yet as we've seen, the rhetoric of individual faith is more Protestant than Catholic. So Hitler offers a synthesis of secularized Catholicism and secularized Protestantism: an intense faith-drama creates a new organic religious culture. (This echoes Hegel's idea of the movement from alienated individualism to cohesive community.)

The race must be restored by the virtue of "readiness to obey the call of duty (*Pflichter-fullung*)" (*ibid.*: 123). It needs:

the strength produced by self-confidence ... Through bodily strength and skill the youth must recover faith in the unconquerableness of his nation ... Only by an immense output of national will-power, thirst for freedom and passionate devotion can we restore what has been missing in us. (*Ibid.*: 162)

He wants a restoration of corporate confidence, pride. But as yet Germany, under the Weimar Republic, is unworthy of pride. "Not until a nation is sound in all its parts, body and soul, can the joy of belonging to it rightly swell to that high feeling which we call 'national pride'" (*ibid.*: 169). So he calls his fellow Germans to have a faith that will in due course become pride. It is important to note that this is a corruption of Christian faith, which does not gain substance and solidity from an emergent form of worldly power; it has to remain *faith*. It should also be said that Hitler is copying this logic from Marxism, which is also a form of faith that wants political violence to substantiate it; it wants to mutate into pride. Perhaps this is the very core of Hitler's motivation: Judaism has spawned a "faith" that seeks power through violence, and we must respond with an authentically national version of this.

His attitude to reason is interesting. The truth of his ideology is too deep for the intellectual class to grasp. This class will be replaced by the revolution, for it lacks "the essential will-power" to be of use (*ibid.*: 170). He then refers to the Nazi party's manifesto, in twenty-five theses. "To some extent they are a confession of political faith": whether or not they are exactly true, they must be advocated as if they are. To worry about their truth would lead to endless sterile debates.

Much may be learned from the Roman Catholic Church. Though the body of its doctrine clashes with exact science and research on many points – unnecessarily in certain respects – the Church is not prepared to sacrifice a single syllable of its doctrines. It has realized very correctly that its power of resistance depends not on being more or less in harmony with the scientific events of the moment – which are, as a matter of fact, always altering – but rather on clinging firmly to dogmas once laid down, which on the whole do express the character of the faith. As a consequence the Church stands firmer than ever before.   (*Ibid.*: 184)

What matters is not whether his ideology strikes people as rational, but whether it wins their hearts. And it might actually *help* if there is a perceived conflict with reason, for that means that faith will be involved. This is how people have a really intimate relationship with what they believe: when reasoning is trumped by a sense that an authoritative institution, whether Church or party, is to be *trusted*.

So Nazi faith is influenced by various things: the inner drama of Protestant faith, the Hegelian idea that this alienation must be overcome in the creation of new social harmony, the institutional authority of Roman Catholicism and the Marxist assumption that faith in a new order can be made real by violent action.

Two more philosophers

To some early-twentieth-century thinkers, this age of irrationalism and pseudo-science had to be countered by a more stringently logical approach to philosophy. One of these was Ludwig Wittgenstein. He helped to inspire "logical positivism", a starkly anti-metaphysical school of thought that seemed to suggest that everything was either logically verifiable or nonsense. He was suspicious not just of religion but of every ideology with a religious aura.

But during the 1930s he made a remarkable move, a sharp U-turn from the rationalist assumptions of philosophy. He suddenly saw rationalism as a strange prejudice that infected philosophy. Why should we desire human beings to be rationalist machines? Instead of itching for some rationalist utopia, why couldn't philosophy reflect on the reality of human life? The key insight came from anthropology: we are like the "primitives" we study. Like Nietzsche (but very differently) he stood up to the arrogance of the Enlightenment, and said: actually, why should we assume that our worldview is meant to become increasingly rationalist? This is not because he was arguing for religion: he was arguing for more honesty about what human beings are like. His focus was language. The fact is that we use language in various different ways; it is embedded in daily life, in things we do. For example, we pray, or many of us do. Is this way of using language "wrong" because it cannot be rationally justified? He told rationalists to stay away from religion: show some humility before a phenomenon whose surface they could only scratch at, unhelpfully. And he advised theologians to stay away from the whole tradition of rational proofs, from claims of reasonability. This whole approach to theology – which was most of theology – muddied the waters. He therefore revived the theological approach of Pascal and others in a new way. We must stop assuming that religion is something that needs rational justification; we must let it be its own form of culture, or language.

Wittgenstein was deeply attracted to Christianity himself. He made many Luther-type comments on the power of faith to dispel despair (he was dramatically depressive), but remained detached from organized religion. Some of his comments on the nature of faith are very Pascalian. He once wrote of his sympathy with the doctrine of Christ's resurrection from the dead. If he had died and decomposed like a normal man, then it's impossible to believe that he can help us now – we are on our own. And our sense of need of divine help is a very basic part of being human, in Wittgenstein's experience. It is not enough that we can become clever or wise:

And faith is faith in what is needed by my *heart*, my *soul*, not my speculative intelligence. For it is my soul with its passions, as it were with its flesh and blood, that has to be saved, not my abstract mind. Perhaps we can say: Only *love* can believe the Resurrection. Or: it is *love* that believes the Resurrection. We might say: Redeeming love believes even in the Resurrection; holds fast even to the Resurrection.

(In Monk 1991: 383)

For Wittgenstein, it is simply a fact that we, or some of us, have a need beyond rationalism. The intense awkwardness of this fact should not lead us to deny it. We need a sense of divine affirmation, although it cannot be rationally justified. Our need for this is connected to our impulse to prioritize love, to believe in love's authority. You could say that we demand a way of speaking, or a rhetorical idiom, which asserts the victory of good over evil, *and this trumps our respect for the sovereignty of rationality*. Elsewhere he returns to the contrast between normal human wisdom and faith. "Wisdom is passionless. But faith by contrast is what Kierkegaard calls a *passion*" (*ibid.*: 490). Of course an atheist can simply say: we don't need this; wisdom based on sound reasoning is sufficient. The argument cannot be settled, obviously. But Wittgenstein's point is that we should not be ashamed of this form of discourse, rooted in an intense experience of the difference between despair and affirmation. This is a serious way of being human.

Christianity is ... a description of something that actually takes place in human life. For "consciousness of sin" is a real event and so are despair and salvation through faith. Those who speak of such things (Bunyan for instance) are simply describing what has happened to them, whatever gloss anyone may want to put on it. (*Ibid.*: 376)

So he champions the tradition of faith from a new perspective. Let us respect this way of thinking and speaking, which is clearly rooted in a real and respectable psychological phenomenon, of people experiencing despair and resisting it, asserting the triumph of good over evil. Yes, this departs from the consensus of "wisdom", "philosophy", "rationalism", in its passion, its need for holistic salvation, but so what?

Wittgenstein's approach to religion is often called "cultural-linguistic fideism". The word "fideism" tends to have a pejorative aura. This is simply because most of those involved in the philosophy of religion dislike the idea of faith's opposition to reason. This is true of agnostic philosophers, who think religion ought to explain itself to them; and it is also true of most theologians.

Such theologians will see my account of the modern relationship between faith and reason as highly biased in favour of the nominalist–fideist tradition. Mainstream theology, they might say, tends to seek a middle way, which gives faith its due, yet highlights its reasonableness. This, of course, takes many forms. It is currently fashionable among theologians (believe it or not) to say that the scholastic synthesis of faith and reason was essentially sound, and that Ockham was a razor-happy villain, who replaced this lovely synthesis with nihilistic modernity (I am talking about the school called radical orthodoxy). In its milder forms, this "middle way" approach likes to break down the distinction between faith and other forms of knowledge. All knowledge depends on trust, on conventions of trust.

The idea that faith is a special form of evidence-based reasoning was influentially put forward by the Anglican-turned-Catholic Victorian John Henry Newman. His key point, in *A Grammar of Assent*, is that there isn't time to work out whether all our knowledge is rationally justified; in practice we take things on trust, make assumptions that are tested in the course of experience. It is the same in relation to religion:

> Life is not long enough for a religion of inferences; we shall never have done beginning, if we determine to begin with proof … If we insist on proofs for everything, we shall never come to action: to act you must assume, and that assumption is faith. (Newman 1901: 94–5)

But this conflates trust and faith. I trust that New Zealand exists, although I have not gone to check it's really there. But I do not have faith in New Zealand (no offence to its excellent people). To say that religious faith is just a form of knowledge-through-trust is misleading. Yes, it operates like normal trust to a large degree, but it ultimately defies the normal relationship between trust and reason. It says that we must trust even though reason and convention object. Newman's approach says: think of religion as another realm of life in which trust is necessary. Perhaps this line will always be favoured by a Church that is, or seeks to be, culturally central. For the Church wants us to see its authority as a natural, rational part of the social order: no blind leaping required. Indeed, says such a Church, fideism is an individualistic aberration, a turning-away from the social nature of religious truth. We are an old and venerable tradition: trust us. It is worth noting that Rowan Williams's recent introduction to Christianity was called *Tokens of Trust*, and prioritized trust over faith. The leader of an established Church is unlikely to do otherwise.

One very last recent thinker should be briefly discussed. Jacques Derrida has been one of the most influential heirs of Nietzsche, and one of the most faith-obsessed philosophers ever. The idea behind "deconstruction" is that every discourse, every intellectual system, is infected by a sort of bogus sense of certainty, mastery. It tries to close things down, to be the final word. It is pretentious in implying that it is comprehensive. This aura needs to be unsettled by a new sort of criticism, a perspective that sees new possibilities beyond the rules of existing discourses. He tried to show that this radically open and unsettling perspective is always contained within the official discourse.

It sounds like radical relativism, but Derrida insisted that this approach is all about faith. To analyse language in this way is not negative, but radically optimistic that new truth can be found beyond the existing rules. The endlessly open structure of language itself hints at the promise of total possibility, and he even claims that Jewish messianism is at work in this spirit of critical enquiry that constantly tries to make room for "the other". "You cannot address the other, speak to the other, without an act of faith, without testimony ... So this faith is not religious, strictly speaking; at least it cannot be totally determined by a given religion" (1997: 22). Instead it is the hidden principle within all meaning systems, sometimes called "the messianic structure":

> There is no society without faith, without trust in the other. Even if I abuse this, if I lie or commit perjury, if I am violent because of this faith, even on the economic level, there is no society without this faith, this minimal act of faith. What one calls credit in capitalism, in economics, has to do with faith, and the economists know that. But this faith is not and should not be reduced or defined by religion as such.   (*Ibid.*: 23)

But surely the idea of this innate messianism is dependent on the actual tradition of God and faith? Derrida shrugged at this question. Maybe it is an innate structure that religion taps into. Or maybe "the events of revelation ... have revealed this messianicity. We would not know what messianicity is without ... these events which were Abraham, Moses, and Jesus Christ, and so on" (*ibid.*: 23–4). He sometimes spoke of his whole approach as "faith without religion". He wanted to extract the faith element from the dubious structure of religion, with its institutions and doctrines, and insist on its universality. In effect, Derrida is saying that the universality of trust, in all human affairs, refers to its sister, faith, whose full form is messianic. When we trust each other, even in mundane economic transactions, we are unwittingly signalling the possibility of faith in total utopian possibility. Elsewhere he has suggested that deconstruction is motivated by "the essence of faith *par excellence*, which can only ever believe in the unbelievable" (1994: 143).

You could call Derrida an upside-down deist. Like the deists, he offers a universal religious–moral principle, and is ambivalent about the Judaeo-Christian tradition: on the one hand it enshrines this principle, and on the other it blocks it, with its specificity, and its claim to authority. But whereas the old deists said that reason was the route to the universal morality, Derrida says that it is faith. This lands him in the odd position of arguing that faith is a universal, and so quasi-rational, principle.

Caputo has tried to develop Derrida's approach to theology. In his *On Religion* he defines authentic religion as the passion for future possibility, and impatience with the conventions that define "good sense".

> Religion is for lovers, for men and women of passion, for real people with a passion for something other than taking profits, people who believe in something, who hope like mad in something, who love something with a love that passes understanding.   (2001: 2)

He rejects the idea that true religion is expressed in institutional or doctrinal allegiance. "I take 'religion' to mean the being-religious of human beings, which I put on a par with being political or being artistic. By 'the religious' I mean a basic structure of human experience" (*ibid.*: 9). We become religious when we are shaken from our habits of self-regard, of playing it safe, and believe in "the becoming possible of the impossible", which is how Derrida defined God (*ibid.*: 10). Is this dependent on traditional religion? Yes, admits Caputo, but it always exceeds it. Every religious orthodoxy betrays, as well as preserves, the true spirit of faith. "The traditional faiths contain something that they cannot contain" (*ibid.*: 89). Normal religion tends to ossify this spirit, which is necessarily free:

> Faith ... needs to be sustained from moment to moment, from decision to decision, by the renewal, reinvention, and repetition of faith which is – if I may say so – continually exposed to discontinuity. Faith is always inhabited by unfaith, which is why the prayer in the New Testament makes such perfect sense, "Lord, I do not believe, help my unbelief" (Mark 9:24) ...Faith is faith and not knowledge. (*Ibid.*: 33–4)

This attitude of openness could be called "religion without religion", another phrase from Derrida (*ibid.*: 11). But this urge to separate faith from traditional religion seems rather dubious. In reality, surely, Caputo's idea of true religion comes from a fusion of Protestant Christianity and Derrida's thought (which is itself half based in Protestantism). So this approach is three-quarters Protestant fideism, and one-quarter a sort of eschatological deism that wants faith to be a universal human capacity unrooted in any particular revelation.

Our discussion of the relationship between faith and reason in this chapter has been so wide-ranging that a summary feels risky, but here goes. In the pre-modern period the relationship is reasonably straightforward (although of course not without endless complexity): the key question is whether theology can adopt the approach of philosophy, without neglecting the otherness of faith. Thinkers from Tertullian to Luther reassert this otherness, against the confident theological systems of their day. But from the early nineteenth century on, things get hugely complicated by the "spillage" of faith into literature, politics and philosophy, and by the gradual collapse of confidence in Enlightenment rationality. We have learned to suspect that a discourse that claims to be rational is actually in some way faith based. In analysing the role of faith in modernity we have to look beyond theology and engage in every other major discipline, for these other disciplines have tacitly or openly borrowed from theology.

But the story of faith's modern spillage does not fundamentally affect the relationship between Christian faith and reason. Essentially the situation is the same as it was for Luther or Pascal: faith is a response to authority, the authority of the biblical God. Rationality cannot substantiate this: the believer cannot rationally justify his sense that he has encountered divine authority. Reason is forced to take a back seat, which it finds uncomfortable. On the one hand reason is a threat to faith; it keeps raising the possibility that it is all nonsense, and suggests that a fully rational worldview might be possible instead. Faith has to keep contending against this aspect of reason. But this is not to say that faith rejects reason and blindly takes some sort of irrational course. The believer has to keep *thinking* about his deeply problematic faith commitment; he has to try to make sense of it, work out what to do about it: even though it cannot be rationally substantiated, faith demands thought. Reason, despite gravitating towards opposition to faith, has to be employed in its service. The atheist might respond that this is a paltry, humiliated version of reason, for it has allowed itself to be subordinated to irrationalism. But there is plenty of evidence, some of which we have seen, of believers being uncomfortably prodded by their faith into a new intensity of reflection: the prototype is Paul, who is so palpably rethinking *everything*. He might not be a rationalist, but he has certainly not opted for some easy irrationalism because he is too cowardly to think for himself.

5. Faith in what?

Faith is a personal thing. This chapter finally faces that fact. As an undergraduate, studying English literature at York University in the early 1990s, I was intensely preoccupied by the question of faith. Without giving you the full Augustine, I want to recount some aspects of this experience, as a way of continuing to reflect on the complex interaction of religious, political and literary faith in modern thought.

Literary faith came first, at first. The poet who fascinated me was Yeats. I still think that his poetry contains some of the most extreme verbal beauty in English, but aged nineteen I was more sensitive to it than now. And this impinged on my ideas about the world. Yeats was a sort of overripe Romantic, whose aestheticism was linked to the reactionary cause of the Anglo-Irish aristocracy. His belief in natural, genetic nobility was influenced by Nietzsche. His is one of the most powerful reactionary voices ever, in my opinion. Part of what impressed me was his commitment to his poet persona: he saw himself as a visionary, called to help create a nobler culture than that of the tawdry modern world, and to believe in the value of ancient Irish myths. In his poem "Meditations in Time of Civil War" (1923) he questions his vocation, wondering

… how many times I could have proved my worth
In something that all others understand or share;
But O! ambitious heart, had such a proof drawn forth
A company of friends, a conscience set at ease,

It had but made us pine the more. The abstract joy,
The half-read wisdom of daemonic images,
Suffice the ageing man as once the growing boy.

In another poem, "The Tower", he declares: "Never had I more /
Excited, passionate, fantastical / Imagination, nor an ear and eye /
That more expected the impossible". His entire aesthetic is imbued
with this defiant faith in the power of beauty to save one from
modern mediocrity. And there are Christian echoes, including, in
the last line quoted, idealizing "the impossible". There is a sense of
the superiority of "things not seen". I suppose I was attracted by
the overlap with the Christian faith in which I had been raised:
but this seemed more sophisticated, and more dynamic. I wanted
to be semi-detached from Christianity, but still to have an idea of
a *truth*, known to *faith*. And, as we have seen, this is largely what
Romanticism is: a secularization of Christianity that maintains a
central role for individual faith. For a while I was drawn to this
quintessentially adolescent quasi-faith. One of its holy texts is John
Keats's letters, which I read. They are full of earnest professions
of Romantic faith such as this: "I am certain of nothing but the
holiness of the heart's affections and the Truth of the Imagination
– What the imagination seizes as Beauty must be truth – whether
it existed before or not … The Imagination may be compared to
Adam's dream – he awoke and found it truth" (Keats 1966: 37).
As this suggests, Keats mixed aestheticism with a boyish moral
sincerity, and had a sort of faith in beauty as revelatory, as truer than
rationalism and common sense. And, of course, he felt an intense
vocation: "I will assay to reach to as high a summit in Poetry as the
nerve bestowed on me will suffer" (*ibid.*: 88). Because the world had
doubts about his genius, he increasingly saw his devotion to poetry
as a sort of martyrdom. Reading Keats got me worried: he clearly
wasn't a happy guy. Is this where a Romantic style of faith led, to this
crazy melancholic intensity? Was it noble or just tragic?

I was still sympathetic to Christianity but I had a rather despairing view of it: it was the true tradition, I thought, but it had become impossible to believe in, except metaphorically, ironically. I had been involved in a Christian group at school, but drifted away once I started reading de-mythologizing theologians suggesting that it was all symbolic. I strongly agreed, and thus distanced myself from the evangelical crowd, and lapsed into a sort of liberal–rationalist Dover Beach-bum. At this point I had great respect for T. S. Eliot; he contributed to my idea that Christianity's truth lay in the past, for his faith seemed inseparable from cultural conservatism.

So I was attracted to Romantics, and Tory-Christian reactionaries: this vague form of faith, in beauty and truth as things threatened by mundane modern progress, is what seemed authentic. But I also, thank God, sensed that one ought to resist this nostalgic pathos, and affirm the contemporary world. Here I was influenced by the poetry of Louis MacNeice, who was one of the left-wing poets of the 1930s. I especially liked the long poem he wrote just before the Second World War, *Autumn Journal*. It depicts his rather gloomy thoughts in 1938, and his struggle to hope, on socialist grounds. This effort seemed a noble thing: in fact it was only now, through him, that left-wing thought really appealed to my imagination. I had broadly accepted a Tory line: that socialism was a self-righteous delusion, wishful thinking that misunderstood human nature. I saw it as spiritually deficient. MacNeice's voice changed that: he was not advocating a facile or fashionable orthodoxy, but something deeply personal, and something faith based. In this long poem he actually introduces the theme of socialism by means of a religious image: socialists are those who can't quite fit in to the status quo, who "pray that another and a better Kingdom come" (1989: 105). And he admits that his own idealism is a struggle – against his elitism, his cynicism, his pessimism, his depression, his selfish urges: "None of our hearts are pure, we always have mixed motives" (*ibid.*: 106).

This becomes the main theme of the poem: the interior dialogue through which he struggles to affirm life, despite the world's slide to war – to have faith. Faith in what? In democratic socialism, in civilization, in humanity: the sort of things left-leaning secular liberals vaguely believe in. But here these beliefs are rooted in a vivid existential faith, an argument against despair. Towards the end he semi-prays: "May God, if there is one, send / As much courage again and greater vision" (*ibid.*: 149). And he ends with a rousing sketch of "a possible land" in which all are free to develop their gifts for the common good. This idealization of future possibility impressed me, and felt like a sharp riposte to my nostalgic streak. But on the other hand I suspected that socialist faith was rather weak and derivative. If faith was a virtue, then why settle for this secondary form of it?

I started reading Kierkegaard. I was put on to him by reading some W. H. Auden: it was above all Kierkegaard's thought that converted him, that edged him from Marxism and Freudianism to Christianity. I found a second-hand paperback for a pound or two comprising *Fear and Trembling* (1843) and *The Sickness unto Death* (1849); it is now a tattered spineless mess, with shards of yellow sellotape. I started reading, and was soon amazed by this weird, semi-fictional voice (Kierkegaard speaks through an invented persona). *Fear and Trembling* retells the story of Abraham, not as a harmless biblical fairy tale but as the key to religion's dark mystery. It discusses that harmless childish thing, faith, with a sort of Gothic intensity, as if it is a miraculous yet disturbing mutation of psychology. Christianity is presented as semi-scary: when one thinks of Jesus, "one forgets the dread, the distress, the paradox … Was it not dreadful that this man who walks among the others – was it not dreadful that He was God? Was it not dreadful to sit at table with Him?" (Kierkegaard 1954: 76). Abraham shows that faith entails renouncing "the universal", meaning conventional morality; it means ceasing to act according to what society thinks, and entering the most complete loneliness. Every real believer is a "knight of faith", who appears utterly ordinary but actually inhabits the deepest existential solitude. He needs no special gifts: "Faith is a miracle, and yet no man is excluded from it; for that in which all human life is unified is passion, and faith is a passion" (*ibid*.: 77). He knows how liberating it is to belong to "the universal", where noble efforts are acknowledged and applauded,

> But he knows also that higher than this there winds a solitary path, narrow and steep; he knows that it is terrible to be borne outside the universal, to walk without meeting a single traveler ... Humanly speaking, he is crazy and cannot make himself intelligible to anyone ... (*Ibid*.: 86)

The painful isolation seems to be a permanent condition: "The pain is his assurance that he is in the right way" (*ibid*.: 90).

I read on. Maybe the next book, *The Sickness unto Death*, would be cheerier. It's a discussion of despair. Superficially, despair seems to be a rare human pitfall, but actually,

> there lives not one single man who after all is not to some extent in despair, in whose inmost parts there does not dwell a disquietude, a perturbation, a discord, an anxious dread of an unknown something ... dread of a possibility of life, or dread of himself, so that, after all, as physicians speak of a man going about with a disease in him, this man is going about and carrying a sickness of the spirit, which only rarely and in glimpses, by and with a dread which to him is inexplicable, gives evidence of its presence within. (*Ibid*.: 155)

If one acknowledges this capacity it flares up, so people don't. But they should: the cure for despair is to confront it and realize that its force puts you at the mercy of God. The despairing individual becomes able to see the truth in the phrase "for God all things are possible". First he must be "brought to the utmost extremity, so that humanly speaking no possibility exists".

> Then the question is whether he will believe that for God all things are possible – that is to say, whether he will *believe* … This is the fight of faith, which fights madly (if one would so express it) for possibility. For possibility is the only power to save … Thus the fight is carried on. Whether he who is engaged in this fight will be defeated, depends solely on whether he has the will to procure for himself possibility, that is to say, whether he will believe. (*Ibid.*: 171–2)

"The believer possesses the eternally certain antidote to despair, viz. possibility; for with God all things are possible every instant … God *is* that all things are possible, and that all things are possible *is* God" (*ibid.*: 173). I had never heard this definition of God before, or any like it, and it seemed exactly what I needed to hear. This account of faith was a million miles away from the banal arguments of the Christians I knew, or anything vicars said. I needed to hear about faith from a voice of intellectual intensity. Kierkegaard's whole thesis is that the intellectually inclined individual has to humble himself, to choose the simplicity of faith – which he naturally hates the idea of, seeking sophistication. I felt I was being initiated into an alternative aesthetic, a new way of feeling. It meant acknowledging the authority of God, accepting the need for a new and difficult sensibility of obedience, gratitude, trust. It might seem odd to be attracted to such a bleak account of religious truth. Yet I needed a sense of God as "wholly other": not just the nice idea of a bunch of do-gooders, but real, forceful. Through Kierkegaard I acquired a new, weightier image of divine authority, and its power to overcome angst, to bring order. My assumption that I was moving away from religion was overturned. I suppose I made a sort of psychological decision to accept the idea of God's authority, a decision that felt out of my hands, made for me. "All things are possible with God": this phrase seemed sort of *effective*. Faith was the cure for nostalgia, gloom, isolation. It was the right attitude. I also read G. K. Chesterton's book *Orthodoxy* and was impressed by the note of affirmation, joy and, above all, gratitude for creation.

I was also influenced by the psychological precision and power of George Herbert's poetry. Beneath the Sunday-school surface, some of his poems contain vivid expressions of angst. One of these, "Denial", had a particular impact. Here's the first verse:

When my devotions could not pierce
    Thy silent ears;
Then was my heart broken, as was my verse:
    My breast was full of fears
And disorder ...

The angst continues until the last verse, when he prays that God will "mend my rhyme". For Herbert, the believer *struggles* to have faith, to feel glad, to feel assured. It's a sort of act. He has to keep telling himself about this voice of redeeming affirmation, performing it for himself. So faith does not exactly cure angst, but it defines it, makes sense of it, announces its final fate.

So Kierkegaard, Herbert and others persuaded me of the superiority of this psychological idiom. Did that mean I now "believed"? Well, I didn't suddenly have a quasi-philosophical sense of God's existence, or even a consistent emotional or psychological sense of it. What I gained was a sense that the linguistic tradition of God could be taken fully seriously. The idea of his authority could be, and had to be, accommodated, although it was so hard to defend, to make sense of. Years later I ended up in Pseud's Corner in the satirical magazine *Private Eye*, for saying this, as part of an article: "I am not all that comfortable saying 'I believe in God'. I prefer to say that I affirm the rhetorical tradition in which God is the most basic reality". My point was that the whole issue of "do you or do you not believe in God?" is existentially false. What it actually means to believe in God, in my experience, is to take the rhetorical idiom of his authority fully seriously, and to perpetuate it. In other words, a Christian is someone who speaks about God and Jesus as authoritative.

What about my budding left-wing feeling, inspired by MacNeice's poetry? Could I combine it with this new sense of the reality of God's authority? To my surprise the two things started to come together, very powerfully.

This was thanks to Leo Tolstoy's religious writing. I was vaguely aware of "religious socialism", and thought it not my cup of tea, but this was different: so simple and intense. Tolstoy passionately insisted that the Gospel is not otherworldly, but is concerned with the kingdom of God on earth, which is a rational moral goal. He denounced the Russian Orthodox Church as a betrayal of this; it was complicit with the unjust social system, with militarism. So, it struck me freshly, Christianity was about the need to change the world! Not just improve it a bit, as conventional Christians thought, but to bring it to perfection. This religion announced the kingdom of God on earth. It was basically *utopian*. This was the prophetic vision of the Old Testament and the New: the world would be healed, a new divine order was possible! I discovered the bits in Isaiah where God's utopian order is described, and was deeply moved by the imagery, of the lamb and wolf playing together, of goodness covering the earth "as the waters cover the sea" (Isaiah 11:9). I read some other religious socialist thinkers, and dipped into liberation theology, a movement of Marxist-sympathizing South American Roman Catholics. They seemed to believe in the historical coming of the kingdom of God; they saw otherworldliness as an evasion, an alien Greek import into Christianity that obscured the Jewish belief in historical eschatology. So was the aim of Christianity essentially the same as that of Marxism: the transformation of the world? I started exploring left-wing radicalism, which had recently seemed very alien. This was all a bit embarrassing, for I had literally nothing in common with a working-class hero, except for sometimes wearing a fluffy-hooded anorak.

It seemed that Christianity needed a revolution: it had to become the movement that could actually bring about the kingdom of God on earth. Once Christianity accepted that this is what it was for, it could re-win modern minds, and ultimately triumph. And, of course, church-based Christianity got in the way, gave the wrong impression, it had to go. But it gradually dawned on me that there was a contradiction lurking: was utopian Christianity claiming to be the rational ideology of progress, or was it still rooted in a faith that defied reason?

According to Tolstoy, Christianity is in no way irrational; it is the only rational thing. In 1855, as a twenty-seven-year-old soldier, he wrote in his diary:

> Yesterday a conversation about divinity and faith inspired me with a great idea, a stupendous idea, to the realization of which I feel capable of devoting my life. This idea is the founding of a new religion appropriate to the stage of development of mankind – the religion of Christ, but purged of beliefs and mysticism, a practical religion, not promising future bliss but giving bliss on earth … Consciously to work towards the union of mankind by religion is the basis of the idea which I hope will absorb me. (1994: 87)

He kept working on this vision, alongside writing his novels. A few years he later he noted: Christ "revealed a moral law which will always remain the criterion of good and evil" (*ibid.*: 134). We must get away from all supernatural belief, including "the fabrication of the resurrection" (*ibid.*: 205). The idea that we must establish the kingdom of God on earth is "the most precise, clear and practical philosophy. And they call it mysticism" (*ibid.*: 209).

Why didn't he simply opt for secular socialism? Because he felt it wouldn't work. The socialists would set up a new sort of oppression, he said. "Justice and the equality of goods can never be obtained by anything less than Christianity, i.e. by renouncing the self and recognizing the meaning of one's life to be in the service of others" (*ibid.*: 332). Only a rationalized Christianity could do this. But how far *can* Christianity be rationalized? Tolstoy needed to keep believing in God: one must see one's suffering "as something necessary and inevitable sent from God" (*ibid.*: 220). There are many such mentions of God, but he is awkward about them. At one point he asks God's help in resisting the lure of worldly fame: "Father, help me. I know there is no Father as a person. But this form is natural to the expression of passionate longing" (*ibid.*: 255). His self-understanding could hardly be more religious: for example, "if one doesn't regard one's life as a mission, there is no life, only hell" (*ibid.*: 232).

There is something heroic, and tragic, about his determination fully to rationalize Christianity. We no longer need faith, he insisted, for this is the *rational* route to utopia. Yet he very clearly did need faith. Could this circle be squared?

Of course I was partly wary of this vision that was attracting me. Utopian idealism was a basic ingredient in the worst horror of the century that was ending. I had watched enough documentaries on totalitarianism to know this. But those movements were dangerous because they were wrong. True Christian-socialist idealism would seek not to coerce, but simply to unite the world through its truth. This vision of future social perfection had no need of violence. It would triumph through being believed in. The problem was that our culture was so wary of flawed social idealism, of secular socialism with its need for coercion, that it failed to appreciate there was a true and peaceful version.

One of the texts that really excited me was this, from William Blake (the first two verses of "The Little Girl Lost", in *Songs of Innocence and Experience*):

In futurity
I prophetic see,
That the earth from sleep,
(Grave the sentence deep)

Shall arise and seek
For her maker meek:
And the desert wild
Become a garden mild.

This was the basic plot of our religious tradition, but conventional Christianity still obscured it, with other-worldly error. I met one or two Anglican vicars who talked about "the kingdom of God" in religious-socialist terms. But did they not, by virtue of being Anglican vicars, considerably underestimate the scale of the revolution that conventional Christianity had to undergo? What was I, a rather tense and lonely undergraduate, to do about this?

When I started studying theology at Cambridge this was my key question: if Tolstoy was right, and Christianity was meant to become a quasi-Marxist utopian movement, why wasn't this shift occurring? Or was it, very slowly? Many recent theologians seemed half-keen on the idea. They talked about "eschatology" being this-worldly, historical. They insisted that Christian hope should be fully focused on the actual future, on the historical coming of God's kingdom. Did they mean it? On further inspection, they seemed happy enough with institutional and doctrinal tradition; their agenda seemed more conventional than revolutionary. If Christianity was meant to be having a this-worldly, utopian revolution, why didn't the progressive theologians come out and say it straight, instead of carefully fudging the issue?

I was interested in a Marxist thinker called Ernst Bloch, a Jew who advocated utopian hope. He shared Marx's Promethean hostility to religion, but believed that explicit utopianism was needed to outdo it; he rejected the normal Marxist claim that science is enough. He emphasized the drama, the vision, the romantic side of utopian revolutionary yearning (he wanted to recruit Nietzsche's rhetoric to the cause). In his massive work *The Principle of Hope*, he argued that the hidden principle of existence was its utopian possibility. "All freedom movements are guided by utopian aspirations, and all Christians know them after their own fashion too, with sleeping conscience or with consternation, from the exodus and messianic parts of the Bible" (1986: 7). He praises "militant optimism" (*ibid*.: 199). Is he admitting that Marxism entails faith? He avoids the word, and makes it clear that true hope is rooted in the reality of Marxism: optimism "must be allied with real, present tendencies; because if the subjective factor remains isolated, then it simply becomes a factor of putschism, not of revolution" (*ibid*.: 200). So is he advocating a rational hope? Yes, for true "reason" is on the side of this hope. "Reason cannot blossom without hope, hope cannot speak without reason, both in Marxist unity – no other science has any future, no other future any science" (*ibid*.: 1367). This is a higher rationality that spurns the conservatism of common sense, which is full of "petit bourgeois prejudices" (*ibid*.: 1368). Marxism, he insists, is a synthesis of hard sober science and the purest utopian idealism: "in all its *analyses* the coldest detective, [it] takes the *fairytale* seriously, takes the *dream of the Golden Age* practically" (*ibid*.: 1370). This is a good example of Marxism's need to merge faith and reason, in a "higher rationality" that only true believers can grasp. It is the same logic that we saw with Hitlerism.

I'm glad to say I wasn't convinced by this, but at least Bloch was talking up the utopian ideal, the eschatological view of history that ought to be central to Christianity. What twentieth-century theologians were doing the same? Some seemed to flirt with this approach.

Foremost among them was the Swiss Protestant Karl Barth. In the 1920s he came out with a new sort of theology, based on religious socialism – or was it a reaction against it? He spoke, very powerfully, of "God's revolution", which was beyond the grasp of mere socialism. We ought to yearn for the revolution that will miraculously rectify humanity. So did he want Christianity to change the world, or was he dressing the old other-worldly version in a dashing contemporary disguise?

The more I read Barth, the more I accepted his basic point. Most religious socialism was far too close to a vague liberal humanism. It subscribed to the myth of natural progress, and added God on. It was far too influenced by the whole deist tradition we have traced: the Enlightenment idea that a rational version of Christianity can replace the old superstitious one. Barth countered this with a rhetoric reminiscent of Luther's. God's revolution is *God's*! It is out of our hands. We cannot bring his kingdom for him. It is a miracle, a gift. He redeems us through his scarcely imaginable victory over all negative powers (Barth likes to present this event as God saying yes to humanity). It all happens by his free grace. And he revived a traditional emphasis on sin. The point of the doctrine of the Fall is that it means that true and final goodness can come *only* through God's miraculous action, for we lack the capacity: we are naturally prone to evil.

My recent thought, I gradually admitted, had been Pelagian: falsely trusting in the human capacity to do what only God can do. I had been thinking of Christianity as the way in which the natural goodness of humanity could finally come to the fore, mend history. Tolstoy's rational-progressive version of faith was chimerical. If one is to affirm this tradition, of God saving us, and bringing his kingdom, one must admit that one has left rationalism behind. One can still believe in a good future, a utopian consummation of history, but it must come by God's grace. In other words, when one speaks of this hope, one must admit one is inhabiting this myth of

God's creation and redemption of the world. It cannot be presented as the truly rational ideology with which we can save the world. If one tries to present it thus, one is taking away the necessity for God, and for faith. So Barth renewed the insight that Kierkegaard had given me: Christianity is faith based all the way down, and we moderns are always tempted to try to make it more reasonable. To put it differently, one has to be fully postmodern, and accept that one is speaking from within this cultural-linguistic idiom.

So I moved away from the idea that Christianity is the means to a rational-historical end, and that it must be demythologized, turned into a religion of human progress. The hope for God's kingdom can't be fully equated with historical utopia, for that suggests that the ideal is available to the secular imagination, that it can be demythologized. It can't be: we need to believe in "death's defeat", and in the back-dating of salvation to all the innocents who have ever been murdered, which is not rationally imaginable. You can't dispense with the primitive ritualistic imagery of Christ's cosmic victory over death and the devil. This sort of thing obviously exceeds rational justifiability.

But this does not mean that the utopian is ditched. Christians pray "your kingdom come, on earth as it in heaven", which sounds pretty utopian to me. Faith expects the transformation of everything, life's semi-imaginable perfection. This ideal should not be separated from "historical utopia", for this is the best summary of it, and the concept has an appropriate air of excess, naivety, scandal. Christians should aim to become known as those who desire utopia, not as a humanly achievable goal, but *utopia by God's grace*.

Christianity is the only grown-up utopianism. It is the only form of historical hope that is also realistic. How so? Because it knows that the absolute good it hopes for can come only through God's miracle, not by human action. Also, it knows that the absolute good it hopes for is something it cannot really understand or fully imagine. It can describe it only in childlike imagery: even the wild animals will be friends, there will be a lovely party, there will no more tears, broken bodies will be magically mended, lost children will be found, the big baddie Satan will be dead and gone, history will be de-horrified, death will die. The movement towards this has begun; it is seeded in all loving action. But only a divine miracle can grow these seeds, make something of them. For we are not in Eden; the desires of our hearts are messed up.

Why do I call this utopianism, when it clearly goes beyond historical hope? Because it is about real human history becoming unimaginably perfect, taking off into cosmic perfection. And the core of this vision is perfectly realistic historical hope: peace, justice, each man sitting under his own vine.

But isn't *every* account of utopia intrinsically dangerous? This assumption has recently been restated by John Gray, in his book *Black Mass*. He argues that Judaeo-Christian hope is the source of all the destructive utopian projects of modernity. Instead of focusing on the extreme cases of communism and Nazism, he force-fully insists that recent forms of muscular liberalism are similarly deluded, and sometimes just as dangerous. "Standing behind all these conceptions is the belief that history must be understood not in terms of the causes of events but in terms of its purpose, which is the salvation of humanity. This idea entered western thought only with Christianity, and has shaped it ever since" (2007: 5).

He explains that the very first Christians had an eschatological hope: that God would suddenly transform the world, bring a perfect kingdom. This hope gradually receded; Christianity became real-istic about human history. Augustine's invention of original sin

gave Christianity an anti-utopian bent it never completely lost, and Christians were spared the disillusionment that comes to all who expect any basic change in human affairs … The kingdom of God existed in a realm out of time, and the inner transformation it symbolized could be realized at any point in history. (*Ibid.*: 8)

But in the Middle Ages eschatology, or utopianism, crept back in, and from the Reformation on it began to wreak havoc. But is dangerous modern eschatology *the same thing* as the original Christian vision? Gray is unclear. At one point he suggests not: "In secular versions of the Apocalypse the new age comes about through human action. For Jesus and his disciples the new kingdom could come about only through the will of God" (*ibid.*: 9–10). This is a crucial distinction, but instead of exploring it Gray allows it to get lost. There is one more brief acknowledgement of it, in his discussion of early modern millenarianism; it believes that the coming of the end-time is "achieved or assisted by divine agency" (*ibid.*: 14). This "or" demands careful reflection, but he ignores it. He then says: "whereas the millenarians believed that only God could remake the world, modern revolutionaries imagined it could be reshaped by humanity alone" (*ibid.*). This is clumsy, for it forgets the ambiguity within millenarianism he has just noted. In short, Gray fails to acknowledge the *absolute gulf* between eschatology that peacefully awaits divine action and eschatology that uses human force. He has mentioned this distinction, but fails to see that it matters.

Throughout the rest of the book he talks about political movements that dangerously secularize Christian eschatology.

> The Christian promise of universal salvation was inherited by its secular successors. But whereas in Christianity salvation was promised only in the life hereafter, modern political religions offer the prospect of salvation in the future – even, disastrously, the near future. In a seeming paradox, modern revolutionary movements renew the apocalyptic myths of early Christianity. (*Ibid.*: 28)

This is pretty muddled. He has said that the original Christian vision was about a miraculous transformation of history, by God. This was made other-worldly by subsequent Christianity. And when the original vision is "renewed", in modernity, it inspires human violence. But if this is a return of the same vision, why is it now violent when it wasn't before? He ignores the fact that original Christian utopianism utterly rejected the idea that the kingdom could be brought about by a new human order; he assumes that Christian utopianism should be judged by its modern secularizations. Their violence proves that *all* hope for the healing of history is dangerous nonsense. What defines the West is the "pursuit of salvation in history" (*ibid*.: 73), and it is a poisonous mistake, for it fails to accept reality. "The pursuit of a condition of harmony defines utopian thought and discloses its basic unreality. Conflict is a basic feature of human life" (*ibid*.: 17). From a Christian perspective, Gray is making a sort of category mistake. He is saying that utopia is impossible on the basis of what we know about human beings. Well, yes, that is why a miracle from God is needed, transforming our hearts! "All the dreams of a society from which coercion and power have been for ever removed ... are utopian in the strong sense that they can never be achieved because they break down on the enduring contradictions of human needs" (*ibid*.: 20). He seems to think himself wise for explaining that utopia is impossible: he is just dwelling on a tautology. The question is whether one affirms this impossibility as a *divine* possibility. What he really means to say is that utopia is dangerous when human beings think they can organize it. Agreed.

Gray is right to point out that any grand, universalist, positive view of history is at root utopian. Christianity generally claims to be exempt from this, on the grounds that the salvation it proclaims is beyond history, and shares the assumption that utopianism is a secular thing, an alternative to religion. But actually its own vision cannot be clearly separated from utopianism. There is evangelical potential in admitting this, in offering itself as the sole wise version of utopian hope.

Conclusion

In the Introduction I gave a couple of examples of how the word "faith" is sometimes indispensable in describing a defiantly hopeful secular attitude. Let me give another. Imagine that two races have coexisted on an island for centuries, one enslaving the other. Eventually the idea emerges that this is wrong, that all should be equal. But this theoretical insight is not so easily put into practice. For the dominant race is deeply used to its superiority. For centuries it has owned civilization; the other race, known as the under-race, seems relatively barbaric. And here is the crucial point: the evidence seems to support this. When the under-race is granted some freedom it tends to go badly; they sometimes even revert to cannibalism. The evidence suggests that the under-race is made for subservience. If the old order ends, the evidence suggests that civilization will be overrun by barbarism. Similarly, leaders of the under-race are divided: peaceful co-existence will not work, say some, for the oppressing race is not capable of seeing us as equals. They have always treated us as animals, and so we shall never be happy living among them. We must keep separate, fight them for the land. Again, the pessimistic view seems supported by the evidence, by centuries of it.

How can the island move to a just new order? Only by a leap of imagination on both sides that puts a positive ideal before all the negative evidence. Even once the new constitution is written, there is still a need for faith if the two races are to integrate, to create a viable society. For the centuries of mutual suspicion have not been magicked away; pessimism and suspicion will feel like *realism*.

So what is this "faith" that is required for the island's reinvention? An atheist would say that it is nothing to do with religion: it is a visionary optimism, which has science and rational morality on its side. But in practice it is the conservative pessimists who have stronger claim to respecting the evidence, the facts, realism. The science of the ancient Greeks didn't tell them that slavery was wrong: it told them it was a natural fact. And modern science has often served racism: it uses "the facts" to show that races have different strengths. As Pascal insisted, reason is habitually manipulated by the powers that be. It won't make us truthful. It doesn't bring charity within itself.

So faith could be defined as belief in a possible future that refuses to be bound by the evidence about what seems to be actually possible. It knows that reason is no saving force, for it is happy to serve conventional wisdom. It knows that an imaginative leap is necessary. According to Wittgenstein, "To believe in God means to see that the facts of the world are not the end of the matter" (in Monk 1991: 141). This is the essence of faith: the refusal to make a strictly evidence-based appraisal of reality. New and better things are possible, whatever common sense thinks.

But there is something unreal about trying to define faith in this general way. For the "secular" concept is clearly a piece of religious spillage. That is why our atheists are so keen to shut down the wider, positive associations of faith; they rightly sense that these positive associations cannot be convincingly secularized for they are religiously owned. As we saw in Chapter 2, the concept of faith is still pertinent in discussing political and economic hope, and psychology. Perhaps politics offers the clearest evidence that faith is something we still need, and that it is still connected to its religious roots. We value leaders who help us to believe in a better future; in a sense they are shamans of social hope, which seems to be a necessary fuel for society. And it is striking that the most effective hope-shamans of recent years have been conspicuously

Christian. Tony Blair is the most obvious pre-Obama example, and indeed the afterlife of socialism that he embodied is a particularly pure instance of what we are talking about. After the demise of socialist dogma about common ownership, the socialist vision becomes more like a religion, dependent on belief. Blair was essentially promising socialism by faith alone, without the old dogmas and legalism of that quintessentially "works-based" religion. When Gordon Brown succeeded him, he felt it necessary to highlight his own debt to Christianity, an acknowledgement that this form of politics is faith based. Although Britain very largely spurns religious observance, it wants its politics to be rooted in religious idealism. Obama's presidency is likely to strengthen this dynamic.

My account of faith and reason has been sympathetic to the tradition known as fideism, which warns against rationalism and theology chumming up. Is Christianity hostile to reason? It has a *defensive* hostility: faith is hostile to reason when reason claims to be the master discourse, which makes the discourse of faith illegitimate. And reason does seem to entail this claim. Never more obviously than today, science demands to be *the* explainer of the world. A way of thinking that threatens its sovereignty must be mocked and demolished, it seems to think. To some extent the militant stance of scientific atheism is justified, most obviously when religion teaches false science in the form of creationism. But in general it is not justified: it is not for scientists to pass judgement on whether there is any worth in my decision to say the Lord's Prayer. And when they do pass such judgement, they contribute to a nervously defensive mentality in religious culture.

Whether or not Christian faith is at odds with reason is a secondary question. The primary question is simply: what is it? Christian faith seems to me to be composed of two things. It entails a belief in future possibility that resembles (but exceeds) utopian socialism. And it entails an awareness that we need God's help. It is not really intelligible to someone who (a) fails to desire utopia, and (b) has no sense that we need delivering from despair. This phenomenon cannot be de-mythologized, rationalized; it is not a rationally defensible position to hold that all will somehow be well thanks to some sort of divine victory over evil. Christians must accept the embarrassment of this, but the burden is light.

Christian faith is an attitude of radical affirmation that no form of cleverness can reach, or substantiate. Compared to faith, philosophical wisdom is conservative and intellectually elitist; it assumes that the right attitude is something that sages can train themselves in, but can no more be mastered by ordinary folk than opera singing or quantum physics. Kierkegaard was adamant that faith is an entirely different ball-game from Socratic wisdom. This insight is echoed in the following passage from Žižek:

> Against the pagan and/or Gnostic Wisdom which celebrates the (re)discovery of one's true Self – the return to it, the realization of its potentials or whatsoever – Christianity calls upon us to thoroughly reinvent ourselves … One is almost tempted to put it in the terms of the paraphrase of Marx's "thesis 11": "Philosophers have been teaching us only how to discover (remember) our true Self, but the point is to change it." And THIS Christian legacy, often obfuscated, is today more precious than ever.   (2001: 148–9)

Christian faith is a sort of perfectionism; it desires a new order that is absolutely good, and it trusts that God is bringing it. This is problematic on two levels. Intellectually, it is difficult or, rather, impossible to explain why this divine new order originates in Jesus Christ, and how it will triumph: history and metaphysics form a bewildering blur. One is left clutching bits of childlike poetic language, about death's defeat, Christ's victory. And psychologically, or existentially, it is difficult or, rather, impossible to maintain this radically positive attitude, this trust that all will be well. One is not naturally full of hope and charity, and sunny gratitude for creation; one naturally emits anxiety, and various flavours of scorn, and irritable ingratitude. To have Christian faith is therefore to know inner conflict, on both intellectual and existential grounds. Why bother? Because this strange tradition seems, to the believer, the only hope. Only in this dark, broken language can we really affirm life.

The idealistic agnostic might say: what is wrong with my non-religious version of faith – a defiant hope that we can save the planet from destruction, build a fairer world, and finally learn to live in peace? Nothing is wrong with this, but some of us cannot imagine these outcomes without reference to divine miracle. Indeed, we cannot even imagine our own lives going well without help from God, for faith is not just about hoping for these vague global things, but relates to one's own more immediate predicament. Faith is a sense of total global idealism that extends even to oneself. And, crucially, one admits that one is a barrier to the revolution that is needed. Of course there is no proving that the religious idiom is right or necessary: it is a style that might or might not seem attractive to you. Beware, it might grow on you.

Although Christianity is about as faith based as it is possible for a religion to be, it contains a small but significant note of caution about faith. There is something that is superior to this passion for salvation: the duty to behave lovingly. In Jesus's parable of final judgement, it is not the purity of your religious passion that decides your fate but whether you tried to alleviate the suffering of your fellows. And perhaps Paul's greatest moment is when he lays aside his passionate focus on faith, and recalls what it is for. There is one thing even greater than faith and hope, which are too subjective and theoretical to be without dangers (and what dangers). Only love is unambiguously good. Take all hymns to faith with this pinch of salt.

Further reading

For many of us, literature is the way in to reflection on the concept of faith. *The English Poems of George Herbert* (London: Everyman, 1974) is essential reading for an understanding of the inner conflict that Protestant faith entails. A prose version of this inner conflict is found in John Bunyan's *Grace Abounding to the Chief of Sinners* (Harmondsworth: Penguin, 1987). My own recent book *Milton's Vision: The Birth of Christian Liberty* is highly recommended (Hobson 2008). Novels in which faith is central are obviously legion: Dickens's heroines are icons of faith, like the Virgin Mary, and his heroes struggle to acquire a grown-up form of it. George Eliot's novels are perhaps the clearest examples of faith's migration from religion to morality and art. The protagonist of Dostoyevsky's *The Idiot* is a problematic faith-hero, who highlights the unworldly aspect of faith. More recently, novelists are warier of celebrating faith in any sense; an exception is J. D. Salinger, whose books *The Catcher in the Rye* (1951) and *Franny and Zooey* (1961) explore a tension between disaffection and idealism that is rooted in Christian faith. Many of John Updike's central characters are torn between religious faith and the pleasures of the flesh, for example in *Roger's Version* (1986). Among recent poets, R. S. Thomas stands out as an analyst of faith: a melancholy George Herbert. Philip Larkin was no believer, but a form of faith motivated his poetic career, as my recent essay on his work suggests (Hobson 2006). It is hard to think of contemporary literature that really engages with religious faith, except to warn against its authoritarianism. In a sense this form of "otherness" remains too other. For example in Zadie Smith's novel *On Beauty* (Harmondsworth: Penguin, 2005) one of the characters, a young man called Jerome, becomes intensely interested in religion and promptly drops from sight. Faith is really too strange for the contemporary novelist.

There is obviously no shortage of theological reflection on faith: readers are advised to go straight to the primary sources to sample the style of the major authors. The most accessible introduction to Luther's thought is his *Table Talk* (1995). Those interested in Kierkegaard might find his journals the best way in: *Kierkegaard: A Selection from his Journals and Papers* (Harmondsworth: Penguin, 1996). Almost any work by Nietzsche will give a flavour of his para-Protestant voice, but *Thus Spake Zarathustra* (Harmondsworth: Penguin, 1961) is a particularly dramatic example. Nietzsche influences Barth's powerful reflections on faith in his major early work, *The Epistle to the Romans* (Oxford: Oxford University Press,

1968). Paul Tillich's *The Shaking of the Foundations* (Harmondsworth: Penguin, 1964) is a good example of liberal–existential apologetics; Jacques Ellul is another good author in this vein. Thomas Merton's memoir *The Seven-Storied Mountain* (London: Sheldon Press, 1975) gives a more Roman Catholic perspective. A good example of Wittgenstein's influence on academic faith-reflection is Paul Holmer's book *The Grammar of Faith* (San Francisco: Harper & Row, 1978). Rowan Williams reflects on the mystical tradition in *The Wound of Knowledge* (London: DLT, 1979), and throughout his work he shows how Catholic tradition is careful to root faith in ecclesiology. His collection of sermons and addresses, *Open to Judgement* (London: DLT, 1994), is his most readable book. It is hard to think of a good recent book by a more Protestant voice, trying to explain what faith might mean for us today. John Caputo's *On Religion* (London: Routledge, 2001) is noteworthy, but might be more post-Christian than Protestant.

References

Augustine 1991. *Confessions*, H. Chadwick (trans.). Oxford: Oxford University Press.

Bloch, E. 1986. *The Principle of Hope*, N. Plaice, S. Plaice & P. Knight (trans.). Oxford: Blackwell.

Burton, R. [1621] 2001. *The Anatomy of Melancholy*. New York: New York Review Books.

Caputo, J. D. 2001. *On Religion*. London: Routledge.

Carlyle, T. 1966. *On Heroes, Hero-Worship, and the Heroic in History*, C. Niemeyer (ed.). Lincoln, NE: University of Nebraska Press.

Celsus 1987. *On the True Doctrine: A Discourse against the Christians*, R. J. Hoffmann (trans.). Oxford: Oxford University Press.

Chadwick, H. 1967. *The Early Church*. Harmondsworth: Penguin.

Dawkins, R. 2006. *The God Delusion*. London: Bantam.

Derrida, J. 1994. *Spectres of Marx: The State of the Debt, the Work of Mourning and the New International*, P. Kamuf (trans.). New York: Routledge.

Derrida, J. 1997. *Deconstruction in a Nutshell: A Conversation with Jacques Derrida*, J. D. Caputo (ed.). New York: Fordham University Press.

Eagleton, T. 2007. *The Meaning of Life*. Oxford: Oxford University Press.

Ehrenreich, B. 2008. "How Positive Thinking Wrecked the Economy". http://ehrenreich.blogs.com/barbaras_blog/2008/09/how-positive-thinking-wrecked-the-economy.html (accessed August 2009).

Gilmour, I. 1992. *Dancing with Dogma: Britain under Thatcherism*. London: Simon & Schuster.

Goodchild, P. 2002. *Capitalism and Religion: the Price of Piety*. London: Routledge.

Gray, J. 2007. *Black Mass: Apocalyptic Religion and the Death of Utopia*. Harmondsworth: Penguin.

Grayling, A. C. 2007. *Against All Gods*. London: Oberon.

Harris, S. 2004. *The End of Faith: Religion, Terror and the Future of Reason*. London: Free Press.

Hitchens, C. 2001. *Letters to a Young Contrarian*. Oxford: Perseus.

Hitchens, C. 2007. *God is Not Great: The Case against Religion*. London: Atlantic.

Hitler, A. 1937. *My Struggle*. London: Paternoster.

Hobson, T. 2002. *The Rhetorical Word: Protestant Theology and the Rhetoric of Authority*. Aldershot: Ashgate.

Hobson, T. 2006. "Strange Calling: A Theological Approach to Larkin". *Literature & Theology* **20**(3): 301–20.

Hobson, T. 2008. *Milton's Vision: The Birth of Christian Liberty*. London: Continuum.

Hume, D. 1963. *Hume on Religion*, R. Wolheim (ed.). London: Collins.

Independent 2009. "Leading Article: The Humility that Offers Hope". *Independent on Sunday* (18 January), www.independent.co.uk/opinion/leading-articles/leading-article-the-humility-that-offers-hope-1418748.html (accessed August 2009).

James, O. 2007. *Affluenza: How to be Successful and Stay Sane*. London: Vermilion.

Keats, J. 1966. *Selected Poems and Letters of Keats*, R. Gittings (ed.). London: Heinemann.

Kierkegaard, S. 1954. *Fear and Trembling and The Sickness unto Death*, W. Lowrie (trans.). New York: Doubleday Anchor.

Leader, D. 2008. *The New Black: Mourning, Melancholy and Depression*. Harmondsworth: Penguin.

Larkin, P. 1992. *Selected Letters of Philip Larkin*, A. Thwaite (ed.). London: Faber.

Liebrecht, W. 1966. *God and Man in the Thought of Hamann*, J. H. Stamm (trans.). Philadelphia, PA: Fortress.

Löwith, K. 1949. *Meaning in History*. Chicago, IL: University of Chicago Press.

Luther, M. 1956. *Commentary on the Epistle to the Galatians*, J. I. Packer & O. R. Johnston (trans.). London: James Clarke.

Luther, M. 1957. *The Bondage of the Will*, J. I. Packer & O. R. Johnston (trans.). London: James Clarke.

Luther, M. 1959. *Sermons I*, J. W. Doberstein (ed. & trans.), Works, 51. Philadelphia, PA: Fortress.

Luther, M. 1995. *Table Talk*, W. Hazlitt (trans.). London: HarperCollins.

MacNeice, L. 1989. *Collected Poems*. London: Faber.

Marcus Aurelius 1983. *The Meditations*, G. M. A. Grube (trans.). Indianapolis, IN: Hackett.

McCabe, H. 2002. *God Still Matters*, B. Davis (ed.). London: Continuum.

Monk, R. 1991. *Ludwig Wittgenstein: The Duty of Genius*. London: Vintage.

Newman, J. H. 1901. *An Essay in Aid of a Grammar of Assent*. London: Longmans, Green.

Nietzsche, F. [1888] 1968. *The Twilight of the Idols and The Anti-Christ*, R. J. Hollingdale (trans.). Harmondsworth: Penguin.

Obama, B. 2006. Keynote address presented at A Covenant for a New America conference, Washington, DC, 28 June, www.barackobama.com/2006/06/28/call_to_renewal_keynote_address.php (accessed August 2009).

Obama, B. [1995] 2007. *Dreams from My Father: A Story of Race and Inheritance*. Edinburgh: Canongate.

Obama, B. 2008. *Change We Can Believe In*. Edinburgh: Canongate.

Pascal, B. 1976. *Pensées*, A. J. Krailsheimer (trans.). Harmondsworth: Penguin.

Plato 1984. *The Apology of Socrates*. In *The Last Days of Socrates*, H. Tredennick (trans.). Harmondsworth: Penguin.

Porter, R. 2000. *Enlightenment: Britain and the Creation of the Modern World*. Harmondsworth: Penguin.

Rawnsley, A. 2009. "Don't Drizzle Your Pessimism on Obama's Grand Parade". *Observer* (18 January), www.guardian.co.uk/commentisfree/2009/jan/18/barack-obama-white-house (accessed August 2009).

Stevenson, J. & W. H. C. Frend (eds) 1987. *A New Eusebius*. Cambridge: Cambridge University Press.

Tolstoy, L. 1994. *Tolstoy's Diaries*, R. F. Christian (ed. & trans.). London: HarperCollins.

Toynbee, P. 2009. "We will all Remember Where we were Today – Even in Lazily Cynical Britain". *Guardian* (20 January), www.guardian.co.uk/commentisfree/2009/jan/20/obama-inauguration1 (accessed August 2009).

Updike, J. 1983. *Self-consciousness*. New York: Andre Deutsch.

Voltaire, 1971. *Philosophical Dictionary*, T. Besterman (trans.). Harmondsworth: Penguin.

von Rad, G. 1961. *Genesis: A Commentary*. London: SCM.

Wilken, R. L. (ed.) 1984. *The Christians as the Romans Saw Them*, New Haven, CT: Yale University Press.

Williams, R. 2007. *Tokens of Trust*. Norwich: SCM.

Wordsworth, W. 1995. *The Prelude: The Few Texts (1798, 1799, 1805, 1850)*. Harmondsworth: Penguin.

Wordsworth, W. & S. T. Coleridge 2006. *Lyrical Ballads*. Harmondsworth: Penguin.

Yeats, W. B. 1995. *Collected Poems*. London: Macmillan.

Žižek, S. 2001. *On Belief*. London: Routledge.

Index